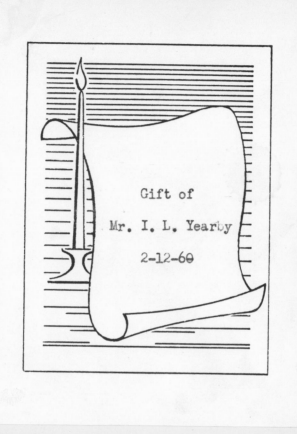

Gift of

Mr. I. L. Yearby

2-12-60

Charles Everett Matthews

WHAT GOD HATH WROUGHT

Through
C. E. MATTHEWS, 1887-

by

C. E. Wilbanks

Published by

Home Mission Board

Southern Baptist Convention

Atlanta, Georgia

This book is affectionately dedicated

to the wives of the subject and writer, respectively:
Nana Mae Smith Matthews and Myrtle Rogers Wilbanks

to Dr. Matthews' staff in evangelism, my co-laborers:
C. Y. Dossey, E. Powell Lee, C. E. Autrey, Eual F. Lawson

and

to the state secretaries of evangelism who labored
with Charley

without whose faithfulness this story would
never have transpired

Copyright 1957

HOME MISSION BOARD

SOUTHERN BAPTIST CONVENTION

Atlanta, Georgia

BP 11408—1500—3-57

TABLE OF CONTENTS

PREFACE

My consent for this book to be published came after much prayer and serious consideration as to its merits. This hesitancy was due to an experience that I had in my early Christian life in observing the great injury that came to the cause of Christ by the over-eulogizing of a man who had been greatly used of God.

The deifying of man and the minifying of God has ever been a weakness of the human race. The Christian world has not been free of the guilt of this subtle practice. There is nothing about any man that would justify the glorifying of him. If there is anything good that man has done for the cause of Christ and humanity, it was God who made it possible. Therefore, the rightful subject of this book is *What God Hath Wrought*.

The phenomena of my life could not be fully realized unless one knew the story of it. We have a complete history of my ancestors on both my father's and my mother's side back to the Revolutionary War. There is no record that any relative on either side was a minister of the gospel aside from a third cousin. My limited training was for the business world. I was saved at the age of 27 and was called of God to preach at the age of 32. My limitations were so evident and preparation for Christian service so meager that it should leave no doubt in the minds of those who read this book that the title of it, *What God Hath Wrought*, is correctly chosen.

The choice of an author for this book was left to me. It was not an easy decision to make. A number of close friends who are capable writers volunteered to undertake the task. Dr. C. E. Wilbanks, who sought not to do it, was finally chosen for two reasons:

First, in my judgment, he is one of the most capable writers to be found in our Convention. Second, due to our associations through the years and his keen insight into the type of work to which my life has been dedicated, he seems to be the logical choice. Any contribution that I have made to the material in this book relative to data is assured to be 100 per cent correct.

Space would not permit and it would be impossible for me to relate the names of all who have made a contribution to my life as a minister, from the human standpoint. They have come from many sources. First, my precious wife and the children; then, Dr. L. R. Scarborough, and faculty members of Southwestern Baptist Theological Seminary; Dr. J. B. Lawrence; the faithful members of the staff of the Department of Evangelism of the Home Mission Board; multitudes of pastors and denominational leaders; and the many faithful servants of Christ over the years who were members of the Travis Avenue Baptist Church, Fort Worth, Texas.

—C. E. Matthews

FOREWORD

The book you hold in your hand is a biography, but it is far more than that. It is the story of the work of God in the life of a man. It is not so much the story of an unusual man; it is the story of an ordinary man in the hands of God. As you read the book you will smile and cry in the same breath at the humanity of the man and simultaneously rededicate your own life to the Saviour. When asked to permit the writing of this book, Dr. Matthews flatly refused by saying, "The story of a man is the cheapest thing I know." When told that it would not be the story of a man but of the development of the Southern Baptist program of evangelism, he immediately began to gather materials.

"Matty" will always be an inspiration to those who remember him as an athlete. The Travis Avenue Baptist Church stands as a mighty monument to his dedicated ministry there. However, his greatest contribution was made during the last ten years of his life. More souls were saved as a result of his ministry as secretary of evangelism than would have been in a dozen lifetimes as pastor. His evangelistic ministry will bear fruit through the lives of thousands of pastors for many generations to come.

Dr. Wilbanks, who knew "Dr. Charley" well, has written a vivid, interesting, and inspiring book. Its illustrative material alone is worth many times its price. After reading it you will be a better man, a better Christian, and a more dynamic soul-winner. I am compelled to say here what I have said so many times, that no man in modern Christendom has made a greater contribution to the kingdom of God than C. E. Matthews. Here's that story.

—Leonard Sanderson

INTRODUCTION

When I received the manuscript *What God Hath Wrought Through C. E. Matthews,* I thought I would take several periods of time to read it. But when once I started it, I could not stop in my reading of the potently-written biography of a remarkable man whom God has used so mightily through the years for the propagation of God's glorious gospel, for the salvation of multitudes, for superlative leadership, and for achievement in gospel evangelism.

This book, the reading of which is like taking a long voyage through a wonderland, shows how in spiritually-passionate preaching in so many places, in pastoral visitation, in personal witnessing to win the lost, in outstanding leadership in matters of our great Southern Baptist Convention, and in daring defiance of difficulties, Dr. C. E. Matthews has been a channel through which God himself has become articulate.

Having been associated with him in his own church in a revival meeting, having traveled with him over the land as we had part in evangelistic conferences, having counseled with him in matters pertaining to the causes of Christ as represented by Southern Baptists, I know that millions would say of him what was written of Barnabas: "For he was a good man, and full of the Holy Ghost and of faith: and much people was added unto the Lord" (Acts 11:24).

One cannot read this manuscript without thinking of 2 Corinthians 4:8-11: "We are troubled on every side, yet not distressed; we are perplexed, but not in despair; persecuted, but not forsaken; cast down, but not destroyed; always bearing about in the body the dying of the Lord Jesus, that the life also of Jesus might be made manifest in our body. For we which live are alway delivered unto death for Jesus' sake, that the life also of Jesus might be made manifest in our mortal flesh."

All of which is to say that those who do not read this book will cheat themselves. Moreover, all who do read it will find their lives enriched—and will stand amazed at what God hath wrought through one man fully yielded to do God's will and to preach God's Word.

No student, no preacher, no Christian ought to fail or refuse to read this remarkable book. No home and no library ought to be without it. Many will want to read it more than once.

—Robert G. Lee

Without Benefit of Clergy

What is the earliest remembered incident in your life?

When Charley Matthews related the earliest incident of his life which he could recall, he let us in on the beginning of *What God Hath Wrought* in the life of one person. At three years of age, as a fatherless boy living in his grandmother's home, he was accustomed to sleeping with her. It was his habit to put his arm across his grandmother's breast and cuddle down by her side.

One morning he awoke on his side of the bed. Immediately he eased over and slipped his arm across Grandmother's breast. She jumped, and he looked up into the startled face of "Aunt Fannie Terrell," who actually was no kin at all, BUT AN OVERNIGHT GUEST. He did a jackknife dive to the foot of the bed to escape his embarrassment. There he remained adamant, UNDER the cover, unmovable by persuasion, by pulling of foot or of hand. He was showing a character trait which lasted throughout life: namely, when his mind was made up, he was not moved by persuasion or by pressure.

God wrought well when he built these character traits into Charley Matthews, for they have leaped out from Panky Hollow, Gasconade County, Missouri, to the ends of the earth to extend the kingdom of God through evangelism, and to win multitudes to the Lord Jesus Christ as Saviour. In addition we can see in that little boy at the foot of the bed under the cover, a type of modesty and humility which characterized him throughout life.

God used Eunice and Lois to give Timothy his spiritual heritage. He moved through father and grandfather, both preachers, to endow Charles Haddon Spurgeon. His grandfather could be in the middle of a sermon when Charles Haddon walked in, and upon relating to his grandson the text and its treatment thus far, could sit down and enjoy Charles' completion of the sermon just as he would have done it—and vice versa. They were identical spirits, it seemed.

Charley Matthews had no such heritage. In him God wrought without benefit of clergy. Among his forebears, paternal and maternal, is found no one in full-time religious work. There was no environment or inheritance touched by the ministry.

Since no man is in competition with another, but can be truly measured as he grows above his inheritance, environment, and former self, take a look at Charley's background.

Charley's great-great-grandfather was captured by British soldiers in the Revolutionary War. With him, two other men were bound and thrown on a brush heap. For some reason it was not burned. Young Matthews escaped, lived among friendly Indians, and married one of their maidens. To him later was born James A., in Franklin County, Tennessee. In due time James A. Matthews, his wife, and three children journeyed in a one-horse cart into the wilderness country of Gasconade County, Missouri. There he traded the cart for a cabin. Indians and wild animals abounded. Taxes were paid with furs, beeswax, and tallow. St. Louis, 90 miles away, was the trading post. The post office, Union, was 30 miles away.

On November 11, 1836, in Third Township, Gasconade County, Missouri, was born Charles M. His schooling was in the typical log cabin, split log seats, wall desks, doors on wooden hinges. Charles M. was a diligent student, strong and courageous.

At age 21, February 21, 1858, he married Miss Jane Fitzgerald. They settled practically on the line later known as Mason and Dixon's Line. To them were born Lucretia, Jane, and Henry A. The son, Henry A., was destined to become the father of the hero of this volume.

Into their home came all the issues from both sides of the Mason and Dixon's Line. But all the Matthews were on the Union side. James A. raised First Missouri Volunteer Regiment of Home Guards, put in $7,000.00 cash and several thousand dollars' worth of food and clothing. He became a colonel in the regiment, and ever after was called "Colonel," or "Honorable James A. Matthews."

His patriotic son, Charles M., enlisted in Company I, Sixth Missouri Cavalry, in the Civil War. He fought at Wilson's Creek, Surcy

Landing on Red River, Cross Roads, Cotton Plant, Arkansas Post, Siege of Vicksburg, Mobile, and Banks' defeat at Sabine, and came out a 2nd lieutenant. An acute disease cut his tenure to three years as a soldier, and left him totally disabled as to manual labor. However, he was elected county judge, 1880, and presiding judge, 1882. He served 16 successive terms. In addition, his 271-acre farm was given to farming and stock raising. Judge Matthews became a Christian and was a Baptist for over 30 years. Jane died in 1860 and in 1867 Matthews married Miss Helen Hinton.

Twenty miles away, but across the Mason and Dixon's Line, lived another pioneer family, descendants of an Irishman named Robert Lucas, also of Revolutionary War record. Robert Lucas, for whom Lucas Avenue is named, lived in St. Louis. In the St. Louis vicinity lived the son of Robert Lacy, young Levi Lacy, and his wife, Eliza Miller Lacy. Their son Richard Lacy married Phoebe Jane Lucas, granddaughter of Robert Lucas. When they moved 90 miles into the Ozarks, they settled 20 miles from the Charles M. Matthews farm.

Richard and Phoebe Jane Lacy gave one daughter a beautiful scripture name, Mary Elizabeth. She grew up and married a boy 20 miles away over the mountains, Henry A. Matthews, February 5, 1883.

To Henry A. and Mary Elizabeth Matthews was born on March 23, 1887, the son who is the subject of this book. There were also two daughters, Omma (Mrs. W. E. Gorman), St. Louis, member Third Baptist Church, and Nora (Mrs. J. C. Fraser), East St. Louis, member Lansdowne Baptist Church. Charley was the youngest.

Richard and Phoebe Jane Lacy reared a large family. Dr. Matthews often said, "I have more kinfolks in Missouri than there are Indians in any single tribe."

So, into the body of Charles Everett Matthews came the rugged strength and courage of four generations of pioneers. They were frontiersmen: proud, rugged, brave, as hard as the rock in the mountains, tough as the Ozark winters which froze solid creeks and rivers; hardy as the trees growing on the mountain sides; their word was their bond, and their blood streams were as pure as the Ozark springs, and could be as cold.

The happy marriage of Mary Elizabeth and Henry Matthews was to be short lived. It was broken when their third little one, Charles Everett, was ten months old. Henry's mountaineer spirit and his willingness to fight at the drop of a hat wrought his death.

The story of the tragic, untimely, and murderous death of Henry A. Matthews, Charley's father, was told by a respected citizen still living in the community, who in his youth was often in Charley's home. Though that death occurred 68 years ago, this friend's eyes flashed as he talked with quickened breath about the dance and the murder, and in less than 30 days afterward those eyes were closed in death. All the Matthews men were musical, and especially competent with a violin. Henry was noted for his ability with his "fiddle." He was popular and always sought to play for the dances frequently conducted over the community.

It was two nights before Christmas in 1887. In the Jose Mill Community that twenty-third night of December, the dance was in full progress. Henry A. Matthews was "fiddling" for the frolic. Pink Harrison and William A. Jose struck up a quarrel. Henry tried to make peace. Pink Harrison invited him out of the house. For a man to ignore such a challenge in that frontier country would have lost face for him irreparably. It was nothing less than an open dare before all the guests to come outside and fight it out like a man. Thus, as frequently happens, the peacemaker became a principal in the battle. Henry stood up, smiled, laid aside his fiddle, put on his hat, and in a silence as deep as the mountain canyons in the Ozarks, walked through the door into the darkness and into sudden death, with no chance to defend himself.

Pink had walked out ahead of him. How he knew that there was an instrument of death out there, or how he got hold of it in the dark so quickly is not known to this generation. Between the steps and the gate lay a pickax, the sharp blade of which had been sharpened to a razor-like edge. There was no handle in this pickax which could dig coal from the mines or tear the gravel from railroad tracks. Pink Harrison picked it up by the blunt end and stood waiting in the darkness. In the hands of a workman this was a marvelously useful tool. In the hands of Pink Harrison it became, suddenly and swiftly, the instrument of death. No feet were swirling now over the dance floor. The fiddle lay silent. Women stood paralyzed or sat tense and motionless. Men breathed heavily and the silence was full of the ominous preconception of tragedy. The chill of death rushed over the goose bumps of all present, as they observed the execution of the code of manhood in the hill country.

In such a moment of terrifying horror the rugged and fearless Henry Matthews stepped through the door into the yard, expecting to have a "fair fight" with his challenger. Coming through the lighted door his manly frame made a perfect target for his antagonist. As he stepped upon the ground Pink threw that pickax, full force. It turned end over end as if the magic twirl of the hand of the devil himself, who is a murderer from the beginning, had hurled it. That sharp end stuck fast in the center of Henry's forehead. Death was as sudden and as sure as if piercing lightning had struck it.

Strong men pulled the pickax from Henry's head and the dance was over for that night. The fiddler lay dead, leaving no word or evidence of faith in Jesus. A young mother was widowed and three babies were fatherless. All the outgrowth of a Christmas dance! A man had fallen asleep and knew not that his baby son would wield warfare so long as life lasted against the dance and all that destroys and makes widows and orphans of the innocent. From such tragedy God wrought in the mind, nerve fibre, and soul of little Charles a precautionary attitude toward the dance which fired him through a long ministry to warn parents, youth, saint and sinner alike, to avoid the pitfalls surrounding the dance.

Henry's body was laid to rest in the Oak Grove Cemetery, which is still used by the people of that area, and is well kept, about four miles southwest of Red Bird.

Henry's young widow, with her three precious children, turned mournfully to her mother and went to live in her house again. Phoebe Jane Lucas Lacy, widow of Richard Lacy, gave them her best hospitality. In this house, situated on the crest of a beautiful foothill of the Ozarks, Charley learned to walk. Here he tottered around the yard and soon looked forward to going with his grandmother to gather the eggs at evening time.

Without benefit of clergy God was already at work, that out of dependence, sorrow, and want, all might see that he wrought out a faith and a reliance that could trust God in any circumstance ever to be faced by Charley Matthews.

II

An Unpromising Youth

There was no future in a daughter with three little fatherless children living with her mother always. Mrs. Mary Elizabeth Lacy Matthews married Henry W. Smith before Charley was four years old. Mr. Smith bought a farm in the picturesque Ozarks. There, Charley, his sisters, and three sons (Lowell died in infancy) born to the Smiths lived until Charley was 15 years old. The farm was on the fringe of what is known as Panky Hollow. Nearby was the beautiful Burbois River, above which, four miles to the south, stood the village of Red Bird. In this ozone belt of the United States the children attended Arthur Springs School and worked on their farm. At first it was "new ground," sand and rocks, full of stumps and sprouts. Charley said, "It was those sprouts that convinced me that I should never be a farmer."

The house stood on a slight elevation with a great spring to the west, towards "the big road," and the barn was on another little hill to the east. Two hundred yards south Charley watered the horses "thousands of times" in the water hole in the spring branch. The big spring could not be dipped dry and in it lived a fish put there by Jack Smith, cousin to Henry W., enjoying his cold haven for over 20 years.

Arthur Springs School, in a frame building, offered six months of "Readin', 'Ritin' and 'Rithmetic," under one teacher, to all ages. Of his home community, Charley has said, "It was backward, typical of rural life of that day in the Ozarks, 12 miles behind the railroad depot. However, from that and other such communities have come outstanding men and women who have blessed the world in every walk of life." In an address, Sergeant York, of the Tennessee mountains, decorated as the outstanding single soldier of World War I, used an expression which described Charley's Ozark people:

15

"One could not say they are not intelligent or that they are ignorant! They just do not have book-learnin'. One farmer drove a cow past another's house. The second said 'How far can you hear that cow bell?' He said 'Twelve miles. That's how far I've drove her, and I heerd it every step of the way.' "

In Arthur Springs School were some pupils 21 years of age who never did learn to read well the *First Reader*, or to spell the simplest words. One of these became Charley's hunting partner. His valued dog was "Old Oley." One night he led Charley along, carrying a kerosene lantern with a thick disk of glass in the chimney making it a sort of spotlight. While hunting they crossed a trestle on the Frisco railroad. They heard that old "Cannon Ball" freight coming, the fastest thing then on wheels. They stumbled to safety as the long train thundered by. When the dust settled they walked on down the track, Charley's little friend humping along ahead of him, lantern in hand. Presently he stopped, shined that bull's eye lantern light on something, and walked on. Charley had seen one of Oley's legs lying on the track. Another stop revealed Oley's tail. Another spotted his head. Finally the little stoop-shouldered one, bending over a dog's body, broke the silence, "I believe sumpin' has happened to Oley."

The last day of school in Arthur Springs was an epoch in the lives of all, teacher, pupils, and parents. It was filled with declamations, recitations, dramas suited to the life and times, and original speeches. No one was excused. Everyone performed. Renewal of contract for the teacher often was determined by the bigness of the day. Always the program of the day was interrupted to gather around an outside table to eat dinner on the grounds, brought by every family in attendance upon the gala occasion.

There were other great social events in the year: the box supper in the schoolhouse in the fall of the year, Christmas, and the Fourth of July.

At the box supper the girls and women sat excitedly watching their boxes auctioned to the highest bidder. They had vied with each other in decorating those little boxes of good things to eat, for sometimes a prize was thus won. The men bidders tried to figure out which box belonged to their special girl friends, or their wives,

Mrs. C. E. Matthews in 1925

C. E. Matthews in 1925

so they could determine whether to bid the highest or the lowest, for the buyer always ate the contents with the maker.

Christmas, then as now, was celebrated with the revelry of the dance with its favorite accompaniment of drinking alcohol. Charley said he hated the dance so he never learned even the calls, "and Mother would not go within a hundred yards of one." It's easy to see how God was working in the heart of a youth to develop a champion of sobriety, morality, and civic righteousness.

The Fourth of July amongst those descendants of the Revolutionary War was the outstanding celebration of the year, outside, under the giant trees of the post office village, Red Bird, overlooking the Burbois River. It began in the morning with hoofbeats of galloping horses as young men dashed around. Then came courting couples in buggies, smelling sweet with cologne. Everywhere could be heard the clucking of wagon wheels as whole families bumped to a rocky halt, with boxes or tubs of delicious food tucked under a quilt or blanket in the back of the wagon. With all the fuss of tying teams in the shade, swapping horses, telling tall tales, shouting greetings to friends across the grounds, seeing that the long table was ready and all the boxes and tubs of "grub" placed thereon, young lovers stole from each other the satisfying shy smile, assuring wink, or a word about a date for the dance. But all this preliminary levity did not detract from the serious interruption of a sudden dog fight.

If they were real lucky there was a hillbilly orchestra, and maybe a patriotic address by some jurist or educator. But for sure, by the time the feasting had ended the carnival spirit was rampant. There had appeared the "doll rack," the "ringing canes," the shooting gallery, the lemonade stand, and the dance floor made of oak planks cut by a nearby saw mill. The barkers at these stands were local talent who drew on what they had heard and on their own originality. It was as much fun to observe them as it was to win a doll, ring a cane, or hit three bull's eyes with a rifle. Who is that barking away at that shooting gallery in the last celebration Charley attended at age 16? Oh, it's Charley himself, with his boy friend, crying "Two shots for a nickel; five for a dime; hit that target while it's in line."

Having most fun of all is Roll Kinkade who never missed a picnic. But hear that lemonade barker. The ice stored in sawdust last winter from the frozen river has now cooled that delicious drink. One's thirst was insatiable as he heard the barker sing out "Ice cold lemonade; made in the shade; stirred with a spade—with a chunk of ice in it as big as Roll Kinkade!"

Everybody finally stopped at the dance floor, either to bounce out there or to watch the whirling sets, always made of six couples, and always the square dance. The round dance with its litter of squeezes and wiggles of today had not yet wriggled itself out of the bawdy houses and the doors of the pagans. The queen of the open-air gymnastics was apt to be one who kept her heels tough the year round. Between dances at Christmas her ma was said to have shouted "Look out thar, Sal, y' have yer foot on a coal of fire!" "Which foot, Ma?"

One fiddle with a second performer to beat the rhythm on its strings could dash the "timidest" caller into a frenzy of shouts and make the planks rattle under the prancing feet. But, if accompanied by a banjo, a guitar, another fiddle to second, or a bass violin, or all these and more, the whirling dancers and the tantalizing onlookers would have made Baalam's crew on Mount Carmel look like pikers. Hundreds of combinations of calls were concocted, or just naturally came forth from the throat of the caller, under the spell of the moment. Hear just one of them: "One and a half; cow and a calf; two six-bits make a dollar and a half. Swing your partner; swing like pa; swing your partner just like ma; swing 'em down to Arkansas. Swing 'em left, then swing 'em right, turn 'em loose and circle in tight." Charley declared, "The calling of the dances and the fiddling were classics worth going miles to hear."

The dizzy panorama of stands, barkers, fiddlers, callers, dancers, and cheering crowds seemed to make some of the "fellers" sick. One was taking cold and another felt like he had been snake bitten. So, together they administered to their ills, one drinking a little "cold medicine," another "a little wine for his stummick's sake," and another "snake bite medicine." All were equally effective, whether hard cider from a cane mill, cider from the fruits of the valleys, moonshine from up in the canyon, or "store boughten likker."

The desired effects were sure to come with repeat "doses" under a wagon, behind a tree, down by the river, or behind a buggy. By

3:00 o'clock all had recovered from either colds or snake bites, and whatever else ailed them. There were two reasons why some did not take a "dose"; there was not enough to go around or not money to buy a little. Those who had been thus deprived of their "rights," however, did not go wanting. A couple of close-up whiffs of the breath of one who was more fortunate, together with the sound of that fiddle, the swishing sounds from the dancing couples, and the heat under the midsummer sun, and all joined equally in the frolic. With the upper brain partially paralyzed with alcohol, the whole being aflame with the excitement and freedom of the day, sooner or later someone danced with the wrong guy's gal, or someone heard that somebody had said something about him, somewhere, some time, and the grand finale of the glorious Fourth burst forth to the astonishment of them all.

"There's a fight!" and the picnic grounds became an arena. It always happened. It was part of the day. It would have been a sissy party without it. It furnished a fitting and most appropriate climax for the day. Seldom was anyone badly hurt, though a free-for-all might develop. It furnished the highlight of excitement for the day, climaxed the patriotic celebration, showing men will still fight, and was in keeping with the true Ozarkian spirit! It also furnished a topic of conversation for months to come.

Charley never fought. He never drank. He never danced. He was not often truly merry in his heart. Such occasions left him nostalgic deep within his soul. He was heartsick for the father he could not remember. Before his eyes, as he watched the bobbing heads of the dancers, there was a wool hat with a hole in the forehead, still in the possession of his sister Nora as this is written, which his father had pulled down on his head thirty seconds before he met that pickax, at another dance two nights before Christmas.

There are two difficulties in second marriages when children are involved: The difficulty of the adult who must live with a child begotten with a companion by another love; and the difficulty of the child who meets every situation each day wondering "what this would be if I had my real mama or my real papa." Blessed is that second union when all concerned live and love as one blood and one love. Regardless of the best efforts of those concerned, often it is a life of maladjustment and grief for both adult and child. Could it have been that something carried over from the boyhood marked the man? Among the children themselves there was no consciousness of not being full brothers and sisters: they were always "brother and sister" in all relationships. But Charley suffered great loneliness in silence. Charley Matthews was never known as a garrulous man. He was deep, pensive, and of few words. The man he was to be could be seen in that boy on the farm, struggling with rocks, sprouts, and many bodily afflictions. He suffered constantly as a child. He had poor health as a youth. Physical afflictions plagued him throughout life. It was true of him, as of Spurgeon, that he was rarely free from some ailment: stomach disorders all his life; appendectomy at 22; adhesions later; gall bladder out at age 54, making three abdominal operations; head operation; throat operation; pneumonia twice (the last attack in 1951); and two severe heart attacks.

He knew no German but sometimes sought solace in worship with a German Methodist congregation one mile from the farm. Occasionally he attended Sunday school there. Sometimes the family heard a circuit rider at Red Bird Methodist Church. However, he did not find the Saviour from his many sins, or the Comforter for his sorrow. God was at work as Charley worshipped with Germans, broadening his attitude toward other nationalities so that he rejoiced all the more, years later, when one of his books was translated into Spanish; and he furnished the body of a book on evangelism for the National Baptist Convention, Incorporated, for Negroes.

There was another reason why he did not dance. Charley was crippled. A neighbor reported that Charley limped until he got his full growth into manhood. A sharp hatchet had slipped from the handle as he and Mr. Smith were building a silo, while Charley was little. The sharp blade hit the muscle, cutting it almost in two, in his right leg just above the Achilles tendon. Of course, there was no emergency medical care to be had. He could not move, so was carried and laid on the porch. Mr. Smith took a needle and white sewing thread and sewed up the gash. Ensuing infection, a running sore lasted 18 months and left a short muscle. God wrought for him a miracle as his body grew; instead of the muscle's remaining short it outgrew itself, and no one ever saw Charley limp to the pitcher's mound, under a fly ball in left field, into the pulpit, or out of the baptistry. He said, "God healed me, as a young man, and that muscle became the stronger one."

Another affliction plagued him from that farm for 44 years. At the age of ten he and Mr. Smith were wrestling a wagon bed into position, when the heavy side fell to Charley, hurled him to the ground and broke his nose, right cheek bone, right lower jaw bone, and neck vertebrae, the full weight falling across his liver. After he had been preaching 20 years, at age 54, the doctors removed his gall bladder and said, "It has never functioned, and your liver has never been normal." This enables one to understand why his work on the farm might have been considered subnormal, and why Omma and Nora often went into the field to assist him in completing a day's assignment. Assignment of responsibility to children and reckoning for failure to "come through" 60 years ago were no light matters in any family, and Charley always did his utmost to measure up.

However, though poverty, wretched health, and excruciating toil left him a most unpromising physique, there was one recreational outlet for him, nature. Fish filled the streams, but he never did like to fish. In hunting he found abounding delight and became skilled in the woods. Even as a friend, mentioned previously, was proud of "Old Oley," Charley's family always was proud of good dogs for hunting "coons" and "possums." His last winter on the farm, at 14, he killed 32 coons, a large number of minks and many opossums.

As the family grew in number and in stature the little farm seemed to supply less and less of the bare necessities of life. Therefore, when Charley was 15 years of age, the family moved, in 1901, to Tipton, a little town near Sedalia, Missouri. The mother of the two sets of children had found her health fading, and had sought help from doctors in St. Louis. One day her case was pronounced as tuberculosis, which in that day meant certain death. There had been a flour mill at Red Bird, to which Charley often took grain to be ground. Mr. Smith knew something about milling and engaged in flour milling in Tipton. With six children, a dying wife, and a business to care for, hardships continued.

On her fortieth birthday this wonderful mother, who should have

21

been in the prime of life, lay dying. Her family stood around the bed. She was the only one of the eight who knew Jesus. Through an itinerant preacher by the name of Joe David, she had heard, believed, and had become a Baptist. This miracle of grace occurred in one of David's revivals soon after Charley's father's death. Her membership remained in Oak Forest Baptist Church until her death. She knew the end had come and told them all good-by. Then she whispered, "Henry, let me kiss the baby." He held little Floyd's cheek to her lips. She kissed him good-by. Having so done she became radiant with joy and fell asleep in Jesus, May 3, 1903. Little Floyd said, "Mother has gone to heaven." That sentence finished shattering the family so that Dr. Matthews said, "We screamed and carried on in an uncontrolled agony." Floyd had heard of heaven from two preachers of the community, a Baptist and a Presbyterian, who had often read the Word of God by his dying mother's bedside. They never made a call without reading and praying. Christian women came often to sing and pray and inspire this saintly mother. How this blessed her, and how she went out to glory is best learned from the neighbors. We quote:

Tipton, Mo., May 3rd, 1903

Having been permitted to visit the bedside of Mrs. Henry Matthews Smith (mother of Charles E. Matthews) in her illness during the few months past, the ladies of Tipton with great pleasure write this brief testimonial of her life and character here. We note with sadness that she has been a great sufferer from wasting consumption, and whilst extending to her sympathy we deplore our utter helplessness to give her health and comfort.

On the other hand we note with much joy her health of soul. We find her at all times full of hope, her countenance radiant with joy, and every expression one of faith and resignation.

The pilgrim, wearied and footsore from her toilsome journey, longs for home; so she asks not to be detained here but rather desires to be conducted to her heavenly home.

The Christian Society contributes much to her cheer, and songs and prayers of the saints evidently enrapture her soul. She never tires of them.

While she lives we esteem it a pleasure to visit her bedside and profit because she inspires hope and holy courage in our hearts.

Now that she has left us we are cheered by the sure conviction that she has gone to be with Jesus, the Saviour, whom she loves and adores.

We hope and pray that all her family may show a similar meetness for heaven, and in the end of their journey may be welcomed by their angel mother.

This tribute of affection is cheerfully contributed by her neighbors and friends.

(The above prayers have been answered and concern fulfilled. The night she passed away, May 3, 1903, all six of her children were at her bedside. Not one of them was a Christian then. Now all who survive are living and active Christians, members of Baptist churches, May 6, 1956. *What God Hath Wrought!*)

Being a complete orphan at 16, in wretched health, completely dependent upon relatives, and disconsolate over the death of his mother, Charley set out to make his way in the world. He was five feet, ten inches tall, with deep, blue-gray eyes and black hair, weighed 112 pounds, and was a semi-invalid. With the help of others he battled to gain sufficient health to make his own way.

Charley had managed to complete the courses in Missouri public schools, which was a great help in his high school work in Tipton.

At 18 he made a supreme effort. He managed to work 64 days on a job that paid him $1.00 per day. He saved $60.00. With his hard-earned money he purchased a scholarship in Hill's Business College at Sedalia. His sisters had gone out to make for themselves their own places in life. They came to Charley's rescue. That beloved Grandpa Matthews, Charles M., sent this object of his love $20.00. Thus supported, Charley graduated in bookkeeping, commercial law, and business administration. He said of this, "God wrought his will and his way then in the life of an unsaved youth, for those very courses led to success in handling all my work in business and later in his kingdom."

23

III

Athletics and Business

In an era when a young man was fortunate to find work that paid a dollar a day for unskilled labor, special training might net one as much as $10.00 per week in an office. Therefore, when Charley graduated from Hill's Business College he gladly accepted an offered position with Simmons Hardware Company, St. Louis, at $9.00 per week. After two and a half years as a clerk he resigned to take a similar position with Swift and Company, St. Louis. His devotion to duty netted him a transfer to Swift and Company offices in Fort Worth at the end of his first year with Swift, September 6, 1908.

An insatiably hungry mind, a restless heart, a weak body which he knew must be built up, plus the final growth of that cut muscle in his right leg sent him to watch the baseball teams in St. Louis. He devoured the story of how Teddy Roosevelt had been healed and had built a tough body which enabled him to become a famous soldier, commanding the Rough Riders. So fascinated was he by baseball that the game sucked him right out into the field. The realization that he had launched out into a new world so exhilarated him that his growth as a player was phenomenal. Before he left St. Louis he had become a distinguished semi-pro pitcher and out-fielder on Simmons Hardware Company team and one season on a semi-pro team.

His reputation on the diamond followed him to Fort Worth. Immediately he found himself a member of the Major City League. He played for many years and had many avid fans. Dr. Abe Greinis of Fort Worth tells the story: "I saw Charley play many times. He was a good amateur baseball player, able to double in two positions, as pitcher and in left field. He was a quiet man, strictly devoted to the game. He was never a rowdy or rough-and-tumble type of player.

But his character traits followed him over into the ministry and no doubt helped him succeed well there."

In 1909 the Cleveland Indians arranged to stop over in Fort Worth, on tour of spring training, to play Charley's club an exhibition game. They arrived just before the great fire which swept from Broadway to the south end of the city. The Indians helped put out the fire the day of the game. Nothing ever had made Charley so happy. He would get to pitch against the Cleveland Indians. Their skill humbled him, and he realized that he had not "arrived" as a pitcher.

He was humbled, but not defeated. No one has ever seen him defeated. He had only learned a lesson; namely, there is always somebody who can play the game with more skill—whatever the game. But he continued to play ball and work hard at Swift and Company.

At the close of one baseball season he realized that the opening game the next season was to be against a strong local team. It would be North Fort Worth Athletics versus The Packers (Swift and Company).

True to a characteristic for which he has become well known, he began making preparation. He crossed his bridge before he got to it. That ingenious ability to major on preparation has driven him to success in everything he ever tackled. He even wrote in a book on revival meeting procedure: "Preparation will predetermine 70% of the success of the revival." Charley bought himself a baseball. Every hour he could spare from work was spent in his room, on rainy days, preparing for that oncoming great game. How can a man prepare in his room for a pitching battle on the mound? That never hit Charley as inconceivable. He learned among those rocks and sprouts at Panky Hollow that there is always a way where there is a will.

He therefore put his bed flush in one corner of his room, banked the feather pillows on the bed to fit that corner, and could hear the cry "Play ball." From the opposite corner of his room his imagination was fired with the shouts from the unseen crowded grandstands. Probably no catcher's mitt in Fort Worth baseball history ever caught as many pitched balls as did those feather pillows. All

25

winter long he threw those balls into those pillows, or to some boy he persuaded into his backyard on clear days. There was only one interruption. Quicker than rain on a playing field, the sound of the footsteps of his landlady approaching always stopped the game and made the crowded bleachers more than invisible. Only Charley ever knew they had been there at all. Would that winter never end?

Finally the two teams were on their respective benches. "Matty," as the players had dubbed Charley Matthews, "to the mound," said Manager Jack Packard. "Ole Oley," on the trail of a raccoon the night before the train surprised him to death, could not have been hotter than was this lanky "Matty" from old Missouri. "Just let one of them Athletics show his face above that plate," was whipping his mind, his nerves, and pounding doggedly in his heart. One showed. The wind, the pitch,—and no swing. "Stee-rike!" barked the umpire. Again, "Strike two!" and before anyone expected, "Strike three!" Three Athletics showed. Three Athletics were slaughtered, fanned at the bat, all! They seemed not to see the ball, or could not find it. So went inning two. Inning three saw more of the same— until, of all things, yes, that manager walked slowly to the mound. The silence of his march beat into the stands and echoed back from the fences as it tried to hide in the corners of that field. "Surely he won't pull that man!" Fort Worth had not seen such pitching since Manager J. Walter Morris had pulled the entire field and left C. E. Weatherford to retire a club from the mound alone, in the ninth inning, March 17, 1910. Morris' action had been a birthday surprise to Weatherford, who was 21 that day. Weatherford had set the batters down in their order. Charley was doing the same thing.

But the startled "Matty" heard these soft-spoken words: "Charley, you know you are good. The folks up there in the stands all know now that you are good. Even the Athletics know you are good by now. Every man on our team knows you are good. We all know that you are in perfect condition from chunking that ball into that pillow all winter long. But that's enough. There are eight other men out there on the team who want to get their hands on that ball. LOB A FEW OVER AND LET 'EM HIT 'EM." When Charley let down they knocked him out of the box. God wrought two great lessons for

26

Charley in that silence and from the manager's outburst, "There are eight other men . . ."

In his pastorate, in revivals he conducted, and in teaching evangelism across North America, he never ceased to hear those words, ". . . other men on the team." He applied them to soul-winning. "Fellows," he'd say to the preachers, "don't try to win all the souls yourself. The pews are full of people whose hearts burn just like yours to win somebody to Jesus. Put them at it." When his manager made him let down and he lost the game, he learned a second lesson: Try to coast or let down on the devil, your enemy, and he'll put you on the run, knock you out of the pitcher's box.

"Matty's" great ambition during those years before he became a Christian was to become a big league ball player. His fans were outspoken in their hopes and their praises. But again God stepped in and wrought for himself. Charley calls it an act of Providence that stopped his career on the mound and alternate position in left field.

He was playing a league game on Saturday afternoon. Scouts from the San Antonio League sat in the throng to observe him and another young player, Sherman Minton, later a judge in the United States Supreme Court. It looked as if his hour had struck to drop the office pen for the baseball bat. The fans were electrified with his performance in left field. It was clearly the star game of his life. Just then a batter flied out to him. There was a runner far enough from base to be thrown out on a double. As he fired that ball with the precision of an Ozark rifleman at a Fourth of July shooting gallery, his gallery went wild. Equally as hot, a sharp pain hit Charley in his side. The second day following, on Monday morning, he underwent abdominal surgery. But the surgeon's knife cut more than human flesh. It cut Charley's effectiveness as a ball player. He could not come back.

Of that pain, Charley later said, "It was an act of God. I completely lost my ambition to play baseball. In that way God wrought to change my life." Others of Charley's teammates remained in baseball and made their marks in history. Percy Enright distinguished himself with the New York Yankees. Rogers Hornsby became the idol of the St. Louis Cardinals, as the greatest right-hand hitter in baseball history, led the National League for years, wound up as a manager, and was named in baseball's hall of fame.

Baseball or no baseball, things were certainly going Charley's way in Swift and Company. There was one top job he kept ever before him as a goal, that of head auditor for Swift and Company. It paid a handsome salary, afforded opportunities for travel, and was the apple of his eye in business. For 11 and one-half years Charley gave Swift and Company all he had, ever watching and coveting that top auditorship. One day it fell on his desk! On January 15, 1919, he was to report to the Chicago offices for a period of training to audit plants there, across the United States, and in South America. Charley was 32 years old. Inside his heart he knew God had wrought a fantastic thing. However, two days before he should have left for Chicago, right in the midst of congratulations and the rejoicing of friends, he said to his superior, Mr. T. C. Acola, office manager of Swift in Fort Worth, "I am resigning."

IV

In Christian Service

The mysterious ways in which God wrought the acceptance of salvation by this man from the mountains was clearly God's doing, and was by his eternal purpose and fore-knowledge. It is in the spiritual side of the life of Charley Matthews that the hand of God is so vividly traced. He was born to unsaved parents. During the period of his mother's widowhood, following her own conversion, she purchased a volume of Foster's *Story of the Bible*. It was written in child's language with accompanying pictures portraying biblical scenes. As soon as Charles was old enough to read, he almost memorized that book. Its influence in his life can never be told. He said, "There never was a time in my memory that I ever doubted one thing written in the Word of God."

The salvation of his mother made her the only Christian in the family. The Oak Forest Baptist Church was five miles from where the family lived. That was a long distance in those days. The family attended services conducted in the church by such itinerant preachers as happened along, or a funeral sermon delivered by some man who claimed he was called to preach but who had no training in the ministry. The sermons that Charley thus heard at Oak Forest, along with the religious impressions which he gained by attending Sunday school in the German Methodist Church and an occasional sermon in the Red Bird Methodist Church, did not bring Charley to a saving knowledge then. However, they did deepen his sense of need of God. Also the death of his mother brought before him such realities as to impress him concerning eternity for all the days of his life. Charley tells it as follows:

I spent the evenings after school during my high school days in Tipton, sitting by the bedside of my sick mother. There I wrestled with Latin. One afternoon while she was supposed to be asleep, I

29

heard her whispering a prayer. It was the only prayer I ever heard my mother pray. The influence of that one prayer, and the memory of it, never left me. Then the Lord claimed my mother. She went quietly, and rejoicing.

His next religious impressions came during his days in business college in St. Louis. When he was 18 years of age he attended a revival service conducted in an old dilapidated building on Market Street in St. Louis. Free Methodists were conducting the services. One night Charley and his roommate, whose name was Walter Hale, attended that revival. Walter was an employee of Bell Telephone Company. He was a gambler. The two sat on the back seat during the service and listened to the singing and the testimonies of the Christians. The place lit up with a blaze of glory and with convicting power when the song leader introduced the soloist.

The song leader said, "I am going to introduce to you Sister _____ who will bring to us a message in song." The name was not remembered, which shows that the person was right who said, "They might forget the singer but they will not forget the song." When the lady stood to sing, Charley said, "She looks just like my mother." She stood there, a beautiful woman with black hair and gray eyes. "She is dressed like Mother," said he, "when she went to church." Let Charley tell it:

She said, "Before I sing I want to tell you how this song came to be written. There was an orphan boy about 18 years of age whose mother had been dead only two years." She was looking straight at me. I looked at Walter Hale and said in my heart, "Walter Hale, you have framed me." Resentment swept me. Then the lady said, "This boy was working with a bridge gang on the railroad close to Kansas City." I knew then that she was not referring to me for I was employed by Simmons Hardware Company. She continued, "A heavy timber fell on the boy and critically wounded him. He was rushed to the hospital. A Christian doctor and a Christian nurse ministered to him. When the examination of his injury was concluded, the doctor looked into the eyes of the young man and said, 'Son, your injury is serious. Your back is broken and you cannot live longer than four hours.' The youth was terribly frightened at the doctor's words and began to cry. He said, 'Won't you get a Bible and read it to me?' The doctor and the nurse sought for a Bible but none could be found. Then the boy sobbed, 'O, if Mother were here! O,

30

if Sister were here!' The doctor composed a poem from the boy's words and someone set it to music, and I shall sing it for you."

The chorus went like this: "Only one word, only one tear, only one word from that Book so dear. O, if Mother or Sister were here." That lady sang like an angel. When she reached the second stanza, Walter Hale began to cry. An old lady evidently saw his tears for she came from somewhere in the audience to his side. She bent over and looked into his face and said, "Young man, Jesus loves you and he died to save you from your sins. If you will only trust him, he will save you now. Won't you take my hand and tell me you will trust him right now?" Walter Hale's chest heaved in travail. He reached up and took the old lady by the hand. Then she walked away. A lump came into my throat and choked me. I said, "Walter, let's go."

We walked about eight blocks to the old room where we slept. This room was over a saloon on Olive Street. Walter went to his bed and I lay down on my bed. I never slept a wink all night. I believe that was the longest night I ever spent in my life. I didn't know what to do. I sat up half the night and counted the street cars as they passed on the street below, just to pass the time away. There is no doubt in my mind that God was dealing with me.

At the age of 21, in September, 1908, Charley moved to Fort Worth to work for Swift and Company. A beautiful neighbor girl, Nana Mae Smith, 16, with dark brown hair and gray eyes, attracted his attention and his heart. He asked her to go with him to a show. She said, "Mama doesn't allow me to go with men older than I am." Charley cultivated the mother and courted the daughter till she did go out with him, "even down to the end of my life." Charley said, "The first time I saw her I said within me, 'There's my wife.' " They were married December 24, 1910. Neither had any saving knowledge of Christ.

April 13, 1912, a son, Byron, was born to the Matthews. Charley said, "I almost worshipped him." This happy little family lived in a small house on the back of a lot on Orange Street in Fort Worth.

They bought their milk supply from a neighbor by the name of Ras Arms. Mr. Arms was a railroad engineer. He was a lost man. His wife was a Christian and a member of the newly constituted Travis Avenue Baptist Church. The church had been a mission sponsored by the College Avenue Baptist Church of Fort Worth.

The little congregation had purchased two lots and had not yet erected a building. The pastor was a Mr. Langham, a student in nearby Southwestern Seminary. He had put up a tent on the newly purchased lots and was conducting a revival under it. Mr. Matthews called at the Arms home to pick up his supply of milk. While there Mrs. Arms invited him and Mrs. Matthews to attend church with her and Mr. Arms. At the close of the service, Pastor Langham shook hands with Matthews and asked, "Are you a Christian?"

Matthews answered, "I am not." The preacher continued, "That is a fine baby you have in your arms." Charley replied, beaming with pride, "Thank you, I agree with you." The preacher then had his prospect in line for the main attack, and he said, "I think your baby deserves a Christian father, don't you?" The answer was, "Yes."

Meanwhile, a lady in the congregation asked Mr. Arms the same question, "Are you a Christian?" He became angry and the two walked sullenly away from the tent side by side. On the way home the silence was broken when Mr. Arms said, "Every time I go to church, someone tries to get me to join. I'll be '_____ _____' if I ever go back there again." Matthews said, "I won't either." Neither man realized that his spirit was being mastered by the devil himself, who always becomes enraged and seeks the destruction of his victim by keeping him away from the sound of the gospel. Mr. Arms later was converted and became the senior deacon in the Travis Avenue Church and Mr. Matthews was its pastor for 24 years.

God did not give up. He was finally closing in for the kill of the old man in the breast of Charley Matthews so that he might bring alive a preacher in his miraculous way, a man whose achievements would continually cause people to exclaim, *"What God Hath Wrought!"*

From that baby snuggled in Charley's arms, God continually asked the question with which Brother Langham had pierced him. When tiny Byron was 18 months old he would follow his father down a little path from their cottage as he started to work. About all he could say was, "Daddy, Daddy." One morning as he thus followed, crying, "Daddy, Daddy," another voice spoke to Charley.

"That voice was inaudible, but I surely heard it," Charley related.

"Here are the words. 'You are on the road to hell, and your little boy is following you.' I was startled. I picked him up and carried him to his little mother who was sitting on the porch. I put him in her lap, kissed them both good-by and went on to work. I never mentioned the incident and my experience to anyone."

However, the next Sunday evening Charley went to the First Baptist Church. The pastor preached and extended the invitation. He said, "If there is one here who is lost and wants to be saved, stand to your feet and we will pray for you." Instantly Charley stood. He said, "I could not resist standing. It was the first move that I had ever made toward God. I went by my wife's mother's home where she and baby were and picked them up. When we put the baby into his crib, I said, 'Sweetheart, I am going to join the church next Sunday. Would you join with me?' Her answer was, 'I will.'

"We opened the little Bible that my mother left me and read from it. I do not remember what was read. Then we both knelt and prayed. It was the first time either of us had ever prayed audibly in our lives. I was saved there on the spot. I was 27 years old. The next Sunday night we joined the First Baptist Church in Fort Worth and were baptized the following Wednesday night by the pastor."

The very first Sunday after Charley's conversion he did not report for work as usual. That was a serious offense for he was then in charge of the bookkeeping division, with 24 employees under him. Monday morning his boss called him in, and without referring to Charley's church membership, snorted, "I suppose you think you are too good to work on Sunday now!" Charley explained, "No, I don't. But God said, 'Do all your work in six days.' The seventh belongs to him." The boss indicated that he would have no more of it.

Charley's convictions stirred him to a rage and he said, "Get somebody else then!" Both men thereupon quieted down, and Charley respectfully requested, "Let us try six days. If we can't I'll go right along."

There was one known Christian in Charley's office, Bill Fuller. Bill asked Charley to join him in prayer, and they began praying in the vault. Charley's office began closing on Sundays.

Soon the work showed improvement as did the morale of his

entire corps of workers. All Swift's offices followed the same schedule, "and all the work went better than ever," Charley said.

That marked the beginning of the effectiveness for Christ of Charley's adamant stand for his convictions in Christ Jesus, his new-found Lord.

During the next three years Charley and Mrs. Matthews were only nominal church members. A baby girl, Kathryn Louise, was born to them on September 27, 1914. With the two babies, along with much family illness, there were plenty of excuses for lack of church attendance, or even supporting the church in any way.

But God knows how to deal with his children according to his purpose. The hand of Providence appeared again. God was working in their lives in his own way. This time Mrs. Matthews became suddenly, critically ill. She was rushed to a hospital for emergency surgery. On the third day following surgery, the physician told Brother Matthews that his wife's condition was critical and anything could be expected. Charley left the hospital with a heavy heart. He promised God that he would serve him from that hour until the last day of his life. Peace came to his soul and he was assured that his wife would recover. The next morning he visited her in her hospital room. He greeted her with these words, "Darling, you are going to get well." To his surprise she whispered, "I know it." "How come that you know it?" She smiled and said, "God told me last night that I would get well. I promised him that we would go to Sunday school and church." On the very first Sunday Mrs. Matthews was able to attend church the two of them enrolled in Sunday school.

That was the heyday of big men's Bible classes, meeting downtown in theatres. Charley joined a class of men. Mrs. Matthews joined a ladies' Bible class at the church. A real innovation appeared in the First Baptist Church which they had joined. There was a church budget and a pledge card to indicate their intentions to support the work of God's kingdom. The Matthews pledged $.25 each, per week.

At the end of the year they had not paid their pledges in full. One Sunday when the family had returned from church, Mrs. Matthews said, "We are going to tithe." Her Sunday school teacher, Mrs. Walter Pool, had convinced Mrs. Matthews that the tithe was the

Lord's. Charley did not understand her language, so asked, "What do you mean, tithe?" She answered, "We are going to pay one tenth of our earnings to the church." He said, "How in the world can we do that? We have paid only $.50 a week to the church this year. We are behind on that, and we have skipped two monthly payments of $45.00 each on our house."

But Mrs. Matthews did not surrender her convictions easily, so she said, "Do you know why we missed the two payments on our house?" "Why?" he asked. "Because," she said, "we did not tithe." Then she continued, "One half of our salary belongs to me. I will tithe it and you can do as you choose."

Charley became restless in seeing his wife take spiritual leadership. He could not bear the idea of her having more faith than he could muster. He turned all the problems over in his mind. Besides owing $90.00 on the house, the drug bills averaged $16.10 per month that year, 1917. At a salary of $2,000.00 per year, it can be seen that the drug bill was almost exactly one tenth of his monthly check of $166.66. Charley looked at Nan and she looked straight back at him. Finally he said, "I am not going to let you have more faith than I have, so we will both tithe." The first Sunday in January, 1918, they started tithing.

They moved to their newly purchased home at Stop 6½ Handley. A well of mineral water was on the land. The whole family was cured of all illnesses. That year he bought one bottle of syrup of pepsin and one other little bottle which was their total drug bill.

Though Charley Matthews had always been possessed of bull-doggish tenacity, he was a very timid man in his youth. He was so self-conscious he would seek to hide behind some larger person in his Sunday school class so that the teacher would not see him and ask him a question about the lesson. But God was not timid; he kept pressing in on the timid man who was hiding.

One Sunday the superintendent of the Intermediate Department asked Brother Matthews if he would teach a class in his department. Charley said, "The very suggestion frightened me so that I declined." But God was working in the heart of a future preacher. Finally his refusal to the superintendent would not let him sleep. Driven by such restlessness he went to the superintendent, L. L. Cooper, and asked for a class.

Mr. Cooper gave him a class of seven 14-year-old boys. Charley was a success in a business office, so he made sure he had his lesson prepared. On the first Sunday he stepped into a new venture, he stepped before the class and felt scared out of his wits. In ten minutes he had run out of anything to say. He said, "My knees were knocking so that I could hardly stand, so I sat down." The boys looked at him with seeming pity and amazement.

But a beginning had been made and Charley launched forth in active religious service. What God had wrought was the beginning of a life which is more amazing as it unfolds before us.

Charley did not figure that he was very smart. He did not know what to do, but he was too smart to be caught like that again as a teacher. The next Sunday he arrived early in his department at Sunday school. He went straight to Mr. Cooper and asked to be relieved of the class. He said, "I cannot teach, but I can push a pencil. Let me be department secretary. Let Dr. Graham teach and let me push that pencil."

Mr. Cooper just laughed and walked off. Charley went home that day and spent much time in deep meditation over his predicament. He did not have it in him to give up. He decided to solve the problem by sitting in imagination in the class as though he were a 14-year-old boy. He asked himself, "What kind of a teacher would I want if I were a 14-year-old boy?" Thereupon he began to pray and to think.

After that the preparation of lessons became easy. He thought out a program of social life for his boys. The boys began to give evidence of liking their teacher and he found himself able to spend the entire 30 minutes giving the lesson to his boys. Mrs. Matthews helped Charley between Sundays with the social program for his boys. Everything was moving forward and Charley was becoming a real teacher of Intermediate boys.

Arthur Flake, the famous author of the book, *Building a Standard Sunday School,* and other books, was approaching his prime, and was the educational director of the First Baptist Church in Fort Worth, where Charley was teaching Intermediate boys. Mr. Flake himself had been a businessman in Winona, Mississippi. He sold his business because he believed God wanted him in full-time religious work, and went to work with the Sunday School Board in Nashville, Tennessee. He relinquished that position to accept the great challenge of educational director in Fort Worth. He had his keen eyes upon this young teacher of 14-year-old boys.

Mr. Flake observed that Charley's class had organized itself into a Boy Scout troop, and that Charley had gone with them in Scout work by becoming their Scout Master. With good teaching, a social program, and Boy Scout work all combined under Charley's leadership, the class mushroomed in its growth. Soon there were 24 boys enrolled. Those were happy days for the class, the troop, Charley, and his wife. He went on hikes with them, and they had parties in his home. Mrs. Matthews found great delight in helping to entertain those boys. The boys seemed to enjoy most the delicious fudge which she served them, and often they expected to see a boy so full of fudge that he could not budge.

Charley truly was growing as a Christian and was master of those 24 boys in that Sunday school class. He strove well to entertain them with God's truth on Sunday as well as to entertain them between Sundays. The sheer joy of it was most stimulating.

God was not through. He was standing in the edge of the sunshine circle and preparing to use a strange circumstance to change the entire situation. After a while he would change Charley Matthews. The hour had come. He was about to begin to make Charley an evangelist.

V

A Call to Preach

The God of this universe is infinite in every way. He is infinite in his authority to convict men of their sins. He is infinite in the variety of ways he calls men to preach. God did not use a brilliant light surpassing the noonday sun, as he did in the case of Saul of Tarsus, to bring Charley Matthews to begin as a soul-winner. He used a bolt of lightning.

One morning on his way to work Charley bought a Fort Worth paper. On the front page was a glaring headline, "Boy Killed by Lightning—Sister Unconscious." Charley quickly looked upon the picture accompanying the headlines. He was startled to recognize the face of one of the boys of his Sunday school class. This boy was returning from school with his sister as an electric storm was raging. The boy carried a pair of roller skates over his shoulder and was leading his sister by the hand. Lightning struck and killed the boy instantly, knocking his sister to the ground and rendering her unconscious.

This story was such a shock to Charley that he had to talk to someone. He talked to a companion on the way to work, "That boy is in my Sunday school class." It was then that Charley realized that, although the boy had been in his home often and in his class regularly, he had never been in the boy's home. He determined to attend the funeral that afternoon. Upon arrival at the house, he met the father of the boy for the first time as he was walking in his grief in the yard. Charley was not in the habit of attending funerals or of speaking words of comfort in bereavement. He stopped the father in the shade of a peach tree in the yard and simply said, "I am Charley Matthews."

Quickly the father recognized him and said, "Oh, you are Grady's Sunday school teacher. Grady really loved you. He was always

38

talking about his class. He would quote what you said and refer to the good times he had in your home." As the two men stood silently in the shade of the peach tree, the people were gathering for the funeral. Finally Charley said to the father, "Are you a Christian?" He answered, "Not a very good one. I am a member of the Methodist church in Burleson, Texas. I operate a dairy here in Fort Worth, and have never moved my church membership. I am not much of a Christian."

It was then that Charley asked, "Was Grady a Christian?" That question startled the father. He jumped. He answered, "Brother Matthews, I do not know. Do you?" "No," was Charley's sad reply. Thus stood the father of a 14-year-old son and the teacher of that boy, while the boy lay cold in death inside the house. Neither knew whether Grady was saved or lost.

The time had arrived for the funeral service. The father invited the teacher to sit with the family. A Methodist minister conducted the rites. As the custom was, following the service the long line of friends marched by to pay silent tribute to the dead and to view the body for the last time. The family came last to the casket. Charley stood by that grief-stricken father and has never forgotten his words. Grady was a wonderful boy, well built, with red hair and freckled face. But Grady was dead, and neither father nor teacher knew if it were well with his soul. If anguish could kill, both men would have died there. The father wept, disconsolate; and Charley wept with him.

Before night of that dreadful day, Charley was on the phone. Before Sunday he had talked over the phone, or person to person in their homes, with the 23 remaining boys. No longer could doubt be tolerated. Charley had to know. He asked every one of the 23, "Are you a Christian?" Thirteen rejoiced in saying "Yes." Ten truthfully said, "No." The Sunday following Grady's death, 23 14-year-old boys sat before Charley. The class had a new teacher. Until then his aim had been simply to please the boys and to keep their attention while he convinced himself that he could go on for the 30-minute lesson period.

Their teacher's name was still Charley Matthews, but today he was different. He turned that teaching period into an opportunity,

39

and then grasped it, to tell them about Jesus, about the necessity of salvation, about the love of God. Finally, he said, "Let's all stay for church and sit together." It was easy. In the balcony sat 23 14-year-old boys and their teacher, every one of them conscious of an empty chair in the midst. The pastor preached and gave the invitation. Seven boys walked to the front to confess saving faith in Jesus. The pastor was overwhelmed; the people were profoundly touched; but that teacher up there in the balcony felt that he could never breathe again if that were all. No, it could not be. God could not be stopped here. He would help in their salvation, so he turned to Claude Howard, one of the three remaining, who had said "I am not a Christian," and said: "Don't you want to trust Jesus and be saved?" He pleaded, "Will you go with me, Brother Matthews?" As they started, the two remaining unsaved boys followed. No one had ever seen such a sight even in the First Baptist Church of Fort Worth. There stood ten 14-year-old boys and their teacher, rejoicing in "so great salvation"—but Grady was dead. All were baptized. No one knew how it was with Grady and his God. Charley never forgot Grady.

God had wrought again. That bolt of lightning started Charley in the work of soul-winning. On the pen-written page upon which Charley handed this story to the writer, is a series of splotches. Could they be tear marks? They are mute evidence that Charley never forgot another lesson he had learned as God wrought through him. It was his first time to taste the unbounded, unspeakable joy of knowing that he had won a soul to salvation in Christ. Instantaneously his whole life was changed. Charley was convinced that the gospel is the power of God unto salvation to every one that believeth, and he was awakened to the fact that he was personally responsible for winning the lost to Christ.

From that dramatic hour forward for months there was a growing desire in the hearts of Charley and Mrs. Matthews to win the lost to Christ. There was in their services through their church a faithfulness which had not been there before. More and more they became burdened for lost people.

What a good time the Matthews were having. Promotion had come with raises in salary through the 11 years with Swift and

Company. Everything was glorious in their activities at the church. Life seemed to have burst into full bloom, but God had another plan. It hit Charley so hard that it seems well to let him tell his story:

The promotion which I had hoped for throughout 11 and one-half years had come. I was to report to Chicago as an auditor. In search of adjustments in this promotion, suddenly I felt a complete lack of desire to do secular work, and this promotion became a dread instead of an inspiration.

I was so upset and so burdened for the cause of Christ that I could not rest or sleep. I could not eat. I did not know what to do. My wife and my friends became alarmed about me. I went to my pastor for help. He asked, "How large is your family?" "I have a wife and two children," I answered. The next question was, "How old are you?" "Thirty-two," I said. "What is your salary?" I named it. Then he looked at me and said, "Stay with your job." I thought that would settle the matter and returned home. But the strange feeling did not leave me; it became more intense. Finally I phoned my good friend, Rev. L. L. Cooper, and asked that he come to my house at once. He responded immediately.

I found him to be a sympathetic friend. After I explained to him my situation in detail, Brother Cooper said, "God is calling you to preach. I had a similar experience. There are only two persons who can settle your case." "Who are they?" I asked. "You and God. You will have to get on your knees and pray it through." That night I stayed on my knees and on my face on the floor until 2:00 A.M. I prayed and cried until I was exhausted. The next morning I went to my office. Only two more days and I was to leave for Chicago. I tried to write on some ledgers but could not. Then I said to myself, "I am going to take a walk through the packing house and see if I can find relief." I walked for two hours. Instead of finding relief I became so burdened I thought I would die. It seemed that God had hold of me and would not let go. Finally I said, "Lord, I give up. I have no training for the ministry. I have a wife and two children. I am 32 years old. The job I wanted is realized, but I give up. Here I am. I'll go where you want me to go, I'll do what you want me to do."

I went to the office manager, Mr. T. C. Acola and said, "Could I talk with you privately, please?" "Certainly," he said. We went to his private office. I shall never forget that experience. Mr. Acola was my dear friend, and was my superior in the work. He filled his pipe with tobacco and began to smoke. He seemed as nervous as I was.

I said, "Mr. Acola, you have been good to me. Swift and Company has been wonderful to me. Promotions have come and desires have been realized, but I am going into religious work and I am resigning." He looked at me and said, "Is it more money you want? There is a $10.00 a week raise in for you now." Ten dollars a week was quite a raise in those days. I answered him, "If you were to offer me a million dollars, it would not change my mind. I have to do what I am doing."

He stood gazing at me in amazement. He was a Presbyterian and that was a new experience for him, too. Finally he gave me a pat on the back, and said, "Matty, whatever you do, I am for you. When do you want to quit?" "Right now," I said. "I can't work." Mr. Acola was truly an understanding friend. He remained my friend until the day of his death many years later. I brought the message at his funeral and related this experience at the request of his wife.

It was a long trip home that afternoon for Charley, jobless, promotion gone, with only an incompleted high school education and business training and a heart that had responded to a call to do full-time religious work. This had been done on faith. Now faith went home empty handed. There was no religious job.

But God was standing in the shadows and working. That night L. L. Cooper came to the Matthews' home, and said, "I have a job for you at the church. It will pay you about one half what you made with Swift and Company. I want you to be financial secretary of the church." Immediate acceptance seemed too slow, but what a relief! The next day Charley went to work for the First Baptist Church of Fort Worth as a paid employee, financial secretary.

The brilliant and scintillating personality of Arthur Flake hovered over and around Charley. He was educational director and Charley, financial secretary. This threw the two together. Flake took a personal interest in Matthews and started him off in a spiritual ministry as superintendent of the Junior Department. Department attendance nearly doubled in three months. He was busy gathering money. God wrought the increased attendance. Flake did everything possible to develop Matthews in all-round church work. Charley's inborn ability to learn methods and the manipulation of organization came speedily to serve him now. The mastery of the field of Sunday school organization and of church finances made each day a happy experience for him, and was a delight to his little family. However, this did not last long.

Arthur Flake returned to Nashville again to work with the Sunday School Board. Upon his resignation, the pastor came to talk with Charley. The pastor chose his staff. And, wonder of wonders, he was now asking this man from the Ozarks, in his thirties, with no college or seminary training, and only the above-mentioned experience in Sunday school, to become the educational director of the large First Baptist Church of Fort Worth, the largest Sunday school in the world. Charley was so shocked that he almost fainted. Of course, he could not follow the illustrious Arthur Flake. Finally he said to his pastor, "Arthur Flake is the greatest Sunday school man in the world. I know little or nothing about church work." The pastor encouraged him, "Yes, but you can learn. We will not let you fail." An irresistible force had met an immovable object.

Charley, startled and shocked, hastened home to break the news to Nan. She asked, "What are you going to do about it?" Charley said, "I am not going to accept the place." "Why?" "Well, I have no preparation or experience that would qualify me for such a position. I would be foolish to accept such responsibility." She said, "Do you remember a short while ago when you wanted to be an auditor for Swift and Company, and I asked you if you believed that you were qualified for such a place? Your answer was, "If they offered me the place of general manager, I would try it." Now, God has opened a place for you in his work. You were willing to take a place of responsibility for money—why can't you do the same for God?" A phrase from the lips of a great Dallas Negro preacher, Caesar Clark, would rightly describe Charley at that moment, "He stood there slack-jawed and confused."

Charley was utterly helpless and defenseless. He faced such a challenge as he had never heard of. Finally he took refuge in the pages of his Bible. Providentially, as he opened God's Word, his eyes fell upon James 1:5: "If any man lack wisdom let him ask of God who giveth to all men liberally and upbraideth not and it shall be given him." Charley had never seen that Scripture verse before. There came to him at once, like a flash, "This is God's answer to your need." Charley accepted the place as educational director and for two years the church's educational program enjoyed co-ordination and healthy, spiritual prosperity.

God had wrought a miracle in giving to this untrained man, now in his early thirties, a golden text for his life. Let him tell the story:

From that day until now I have lived and breathed James 1:5. That was the beginning of a series of open doors of responsibility to me over the years that were beyond my ability to undertake, or that I had ever dreamed of facing. I cannot remember ever preaching a sermon that I did not breathe the promise of James 1:5 before speaking. I never accepted a call or tried to write an article or a book without first claiming the promise of James 1:5. In fact, before making an announcement from the pulpit I would repeat James 1:5, and say, "Lord, I don't know how to do this. Show me and I will try." James 1:5 is all inclusive. It is of more value to a child of God, if properly used, than all the knowledge this world can give.

One of the secrets of the mysterious power of the life of Charley Matthews is anchored in the Word of God written by the half brother of Jesus, even James himself.

But educational work was not to be the portion of Charley Matthews always. His dramatic rise to influence and power stood on those two years of practical work as educational director. They were as a springboard catapulting him into success in the pastorate and in evangelism, because he learned how to use the organizations of the church in winning the unsaved to Christ. Those two years as educational director were of inestimable value in preparing Charley for work as a pastor and an evangelist.

Again the happiness and contentment which Charley and his family enjoyed could not last. There was surging in his heart a constant desire to preach. It was burning in his mind day and night. From it there seemed no surcease. The change from educational director to preaching was a most difficult thing. This could be accomplished only if God wrought it upon the altar of his heart and mind. God let explosions of circumstances accomplish it. These explosions of circumstances and events occurred in the First Baptist Church, where Charley worked. He saw the scintillating and peerless pastor of his church turn upon Baylor University, Southwestern Seminary, and the Baptist General Convention of Texas.

There developed a period of great sorrow, travail, bitterness, and open battles in Baptist affairs throughout the Southwest. There grew out of the First Baptist Church of Fort Worth a movement known as the Fundamentalist Fellowship. It reached out into bitter attacks upon the Southern Baptist Convention, with the pastor of Charley's church conducting sessions of ridicule simultaneously with Convention meetings in the same cities. Mention of that lamentable situation is made here with regret, but it is history known or available to all. It is mentioned to show into what depths of turmoil God had to reach if he would bring out his man, Charley Matthews, to prove through him that God hath wrought even in the maelstrom.

This series of explosions brought great sorrow to the heart of Charley and his peace-loving wife. Charley was caught in the cross-fire from all sides. To be standing by his pastor left him open to the fire from the denomination. To stand by the denomination, her schools and mission programs, left him to the withering fire that could be leveled only by as skilled a battler as was his pastor. All this shock and grief could not put out the fire which God had built on the altar of the heart of faithful Charley Matthews, where God was working to show what only he had wrought, in a call to preach.

Charley was now 34 years of age. He sat down and took stock of his resources for a life in the ministry. He was without formal training or experience that would fit him for either the pastorate or evangelism. He had not finished his high school education as a literary and scientific foundation for further study to assist him in preaching. He could not preach. He saw not how he could attempt preaching. The chasm of deepest crisis in his life left him in darkness.

He resigned as educational director of First Baptist Church and told his wife that they were going to enroll in Southwestern Seminary. That meant that he would be under the anathema of his church, and under suspicion at the seminary. The writer of these lines remembers with embarrassment that his earliest recollection of Charley Matthews is when Charley was regarded by some on Seminary Hill as a "spy for Frank Norris," so bitter was the fight in Fort Worth.

Charley's astonished wife blurted out, "Why enroll in the seminary? Why not go back into secular work? You are a layman and not an ordained minister. You can serve in the church as a layman. We will be happy and we can make a living. You are not a preacher."

Upon his resignation as educational director they drifted into a state of anxiety and desperation. Mrs. Matthews was consecrated and loved the Lord, but she had not been called as her husband had been. Something had to be done. He had no job and no money. Their possessions were a $5,000.00 equity in a home, furniture, and a Model T Ford car. Torn with grief over the situation in his church and denomination, tortured by that inner voice calling him to preach, battling with a complex of timidity fanned into a flame by the devil's telling him he could not preach, magnifying the fact that he had no ability to preach unless given especially by God, Charley was indeed frantic. Finally he said, "God has called me to preach and he never makes a mistake. If we only do his will he will take care of us."

A desire to preach would not feed a family or pay other expenses which would be sure to arise in connection with going to school in the seminary. Finally Charley and Nan sat down to count the cost. They looked at the $5,000.00 equity in their home. It was the old Norwood Homestead on Stop 6½, Dallas-Fort Worth Interurban Line. They had bought it for $6,500.00. A depression was on, following World War I. Real estate was down. The property would not sell for the $6,500.00 which they had paid two years before. There simply was no way unless God wrought a miracle. Charley's state of mind led him to say to his faithful wife, "Let's put out the fleece. Let's ask for a sign." Much prayer and discussion followed. Finally Mrs. Matthews had faith to agree to ask God for a sign. "What will it be?" asked Charley. She replied, "If we can sell this place for $6,500.00, then I will believe that God wants you to preach." "How long will you give me to sell the place?" he asked. She quietly replied, "This week."

The time limit was not far away. That was Wednesday morning. But at two o'clock that afternoon a man drove up in a car in front of that house. In response to his call with the automobile horn, Charley stepped to the front porch and asked, "What can I do for you?" "Do you own this place?" "Yes," said Charley. "Do you want to sell it?" "Yes." "What will you take for it?" He replied, "$6,500.00."

A storm was churning in Charley's heart when the man said, "Get your hat and come with me. I have a buyer for it." Mrs.

46

Matthews must have felt like Sarah as she laughed back in her tent as the angels talked to Abraham, the father of the faithful, at the front door. The man took Charley to the second floor of the old Burton Building in downtown Fort Worth. There he was introduced to a lady who wanted to buy the house. In 15 minutes he had an earnest check for $500.00, a signed agreement to buy, and was on his way home.

The light which shone around Saul of Tarsus on the Damascus Road, in brightness exceeding the noonday sun, could not have been more convincing than the light which was shining in the hearts of Charley and Mrs. Matthews as they sat down again and took stock of their circumstances. God had called him to preach. Charley said, "Mrs. Matthews has never doubted her husband's call to preach to this day."

But only God would call a man with a family, without formal education for the ministry, at the age of 34. It was evident that God had wrought.

VI

Seminary Days and First Pastorate

Having put out a fleece which was supposed to catch the dew of
the providence of God within four days, and then having seen the
dew upon the fleece within four hours and the place sold in which
the family lived, the Matthews were facing seminary. The family
lived in a comfortable seven-room house with four acres of land
spread around. When that was converted to $6,500.00 and the bal-
ance due on the place was paid, they had $4,500.00 on deposit in
the bank. Now the family faced the problem of living quarters on
Seminary Hill.

Immediately Mr. Matthews drove out to Seminary Hill and had a
conference with the president, Dr. L. R. Scarborough. The main
street out to the seminary is Hemphill, and as Charley drove along
Hemphill, he really faced an uphill battle over strange territory. He
was 34 years old. He was a layman who had declared God had called
him to preach, and his wife had agreed to go with him. He knew
little or nothing about seminary life or a seminary curriculum. Upon
being seated in the office of President Scarborough, he climbed his
first hill. That was a hill of disillusionment.

He said to Dr. Scarborough, "I want to enroll as a student in
the seminary and take a course that will learn me how to preach."
Dr. Scarborough replied, "We do not teach a course here that will
learn anyone how to preach. You will have to learn to preach by
preaching." They discussed Charley's educational background. At
that time the seminary was enrolling any student who wished to
come to study to further prepare himself to serve God in any way
whatsoever. Also, those students who finished the prescribed courses
were given diplomas or degrees. Dr. Scarborough agreed that Charley
could be admitted and the family moved from a seven-room to a
three-room house on Seminary Hill to begin work in the seminary

in January, 1921. The difference in floor space and yard really put a squeeze on the family from the beginning.

The seminary afforded a nursery for the children of seminary students, so Brother and Mrs. Matthews both enrolled as students in the seminary. Though he was totally without college training, his previous application of a photographic mind to high school work and business college courses, together with what he had learned in the period of a dozen years in business and two years as an educational director, enabled him to make excellent grades toward a Bachelor of Theology Degree. However, the problem of getting a church in which to preach was a difficult one. There were enrolled in the seminary in the 1920-21 session, 273 ministerial students. In 1921-22, 295 ministerial students enrolled. Many of these were young men with college degrees and some were men more mature with long years of experience. How would Charley, in the midst of all this talent and ability, ever be invited before a church with the view of becoming pastor? He was not only without formal training to which he might refer if invited to appear before some church but was also without experience as a public speaker or preacher. His experiences were those of teaching the Bible lessons to an Intermediate Sunday school class, conducting worship services in a Junior Department, and speaking to assemblies of Sunday school workers.

Of course, there was no demand for his services, and no prospect of his becoming a pastor. The family was thrown back upon the bank account for daily sustenance. A businessman, a close friend of the family, offered Brother Matthews a proposition that would finance the family while in the seminary. It was a proven business and perfectly legitimate. The returns seemed adequate, so the entire $4,500.00 was invested in the business. Immediately the depression which followed World War I struck, and in 90 days the business went bankrupt. The Matthews family was left without employment and without money.

Without income, without $1.00 in the bank, with no experience as a preacher or speaker, with the accustomed sense of security which employment had brought through a dozen years, and the words of his pastor ringing in his ears, "Stay with your job," Charley was indeed dependent upon God alone for help. The family

49

prayed for God's help. Almost before the prayer, God answered. A motor vehicle stopped in front of his house, and Charley was surprised when he looked out to behold a friend of his with a cow loaded on a truck. The man said, "Brother Matthews, I have a four-gallon cow and a calf that I want to give you to help you pay your way through the seminary." Charley blurted out, "But what shall I do with the calf?" "Sell it and buy feed with the money," the man said. Again God had wrought and Charley and his family would not go hungry. The cow actually gave four gallons of milk each day. In the back yard were 12 white Leghorn hens, which were good layers. The eggs and the milk in excess of what the family had to use day by day were sold and the money used to buy cow feed and groceries. Charley said, "Our variety ran something like this: We had fried mush for breakfast, mush and milk for dinner, and milk and mush for supper. The strange thing about it is, not one in the family lost weight, and each was healthy and strong. God was with us in our adversity. He had wrought again for us. We had to walk again by faith." The seminary boasted a department of evangelism, called "the chair of fire." The Matthews declared at their house that they had "the chair of faith." "Along with other studies, the chair of faith was the most profitable of all," Charley later declared. Thus the family lived and went to school from January 1 to May 10, 1921.

One glorious day a fellow student gave Charley an opportunity to preach in a pulpit. That was a red-letter day in Charley's life and was a moment of tremendous importance in the life of the family. It was an incident which remained clear in his mind throughout life.

Rev. P. F. Squyers, a student in the seminary, was pastor of a part-time church in eastern Texas. Squyers found it necessary to miss an appointment at his church so he invited Charley Matthews to supply for him. Charley arrived in the town where the church is located on Saturday night. The next morning he went to church in time for Sunday school. He found that it was a great day in the life of the Sunday school and the church. He did not introduce himself, but went and sat as a visitor in the opening exercises of the Sunday school.

The master of ceremonies announced that this day was set aside to honor the superintendent of the Sunday school. This distinguished Christian man had been superintendent of the Sunday school for 40 years. "Today," said the speaker, "we honor our superintendent upon the fortieth anniversary of his leadership of our Sunday school."

The service began and the aged superintendent took charge. He ran his hand down over his long beard and looked appreciatively out over the crowd. He thanked them for the honor, and then turned to matters in hand. Presently he dismissed the school to go to classes, and Charley turned to the stranger sitting next to him and said, "Think of a man serving 40 consecutive years as superintendent of the Sunday school in the same church." The astounding reply was, "Yes, and he done it this morning just exactly like he done it 40 years ago."

Charley did not realize that 12 hours from then, at the conclusion of his night service, he would be standing again in wide-eyed amazement and wonder, for it was at the conclusion of the night service that the treasurer of the church handed him a check. It was Charley's first time to receive any remuneration for preaching. He could not resist taking a peek to see how much it was. The amount of the check was $35.00. Charley later declared, "It looked like $350.00 to me. I showed it to Brother Squyers next day and made him take $15.00 of the amount. I said, 'I know that my sermons were not worth that much!'"

Concerning the education of Charley Matthews, he declared, "I believe my education was ordained of God just as definitely as was my call to preach. This education and training fitted me peculiarly for what God wanted me to do. God wrought for me." He completed every course taught in the Missouri public school at the time of his boyhood. The schools were not graded. Pupils simply studied books as they were able to master them and as their teachers were able to guide them. Each one followed almost in his own way and with his own curriculum. Charley had not graduated from high school at 16 when his mother died, and had immediately gone out on his own to make his way in the world. Immediately he had returned to the home of his Grandmother Lacy.

However, he had specialized in the study of history and Kellog's

Grammar. He had completed two courses in algebra, and had taken all that was offered in geography, physiology, and masterpieces of American Literature that began with Washington Irving's writings and continued through the works of Mark Twain.

He had finished in Hill's Business College, Bookkeeping, Commercial Law, and Business Administration. While employed as educational director in the First Baptist Church of Fort Worth, he had sat in Bible classes taught by distinguished scholars such as A. C. Dixon, J. C. Massee, W. B. Riley, Henry Ostrum, R. A. Torrey, Leon Tucker, and a number of other internationally-known preachers and expositors. These men, of course, were all strong premillenarians, but they were not radicals. Dr. Matthews profited greatly from these studies and retained the richness from these experiences, as did Mrs. Matthews.

The brilliant pastor of the First Baptist Church of Fort Worth at that time brought all the Bible teaching which he could to the church. He was an illustrious preacher of the Word himself. The entire church loved and studied the Word of God. Therefore, through all the mediums and agencies Charley had received an excellent background of biblical knowledge which fortified him for his studies in Southwestern Seminary.

However, strange transformation lay ahead on Seminary Hill. The president of the school, Dr. L. R. Scarborough, upon whom much of the fire from Fort Worth was centering as a denominational leader, came to be the great spiritual giant who left the deepest and most lasting impression upon the life of Charley Matthews. Charley was associated with Dr. Scarborough for 25 years; as a student in Dr. Scarborough's classes in evangelism two years, always as a close friend, and as a member of the board of trustees 16 years. Ten of those years, Charley was serving as vice president of trustees, and two years as president of the board.

Upon the death of Dr. George W. Truett, Dr. Matthews was elected as the president of the Board of Trustees to succeed Dr. Truett. He served two years and resigned with distinction when elected secretary of evangelism for the Home Mission Board. Dr. Matthews served on the board of trustees of the seminary from which he did not graduate. His brilliant mind and gigantic spirit had brought over from seminary student days the strength of the faculty which then blessed the seminary. That faculty included the great scholars and teachers: W. T. Conner, systematic theology; B. A. Copass, Old Testament; H. E. Dana, New Testament; Jeff D. Ray, homiletics; L. R. Scarborough, evangelism; and W. W. Barnes, church history.

Besides the mantle of evangelism of Dr. Scarborough, which seemed to fall to the shoulders of Brother Matthews, another man on the faculty gave him his most valued and helpful suggestion. Dr. Jeff D. Ray, in the class of homiletics, observed Charley's hungry mind and his lack of background for preaching. Dr. Ray said, "Charley, you learn fast, but you started your career in religious work late in life. If you will write your sermons before you deliver them, it will broaden your vocabulary, it will make you study, you will learn logic and you can be a great preacher in spite of your handicaps." Little did the teacher think that his pupil would grow a church larger than Charles Spurgeon did! The value of that suggestion from Dr. Ray is summed up in these words of Charley himself: "I was pastor of churches for 25 years. During that period I doubt if I ever preached a sermon that I had not written beforehand. Writing sermons was the most practical thing in the way of spiritual growth in preparation for preaching that I ever engaged in." Charley further confided to the writer that he was often writing sermons at one or two o'clock in the morning, while the household was quiet and he could hear the voice of God.

As God thus wrought in the life of this devoted student and servant, one is reminded of lines long remembered: "The heights of great men reached and kept, were not attained by sudden flight; but they, while their companions slept, were toiling upward through the night."

The constant dread in Charley's mind was the ordeal of ordination. Fortunately it has been the custom of Baptist churches to ordain men whom God has called to preach without prescribed literary attainment as a qualification for ordination. Otherwise Texas would never have had Charley Matthews, as a pastor, the Southern Baptist Convention would never have had him as secretary of evangelism, and the world would not have had the blessings of this great evangelist through his preaching and his pen.

However, there is an excellent safeguard concerning ordination. That is the principle of not ordaining a man to preach until he has been called to some specific service where ordination is necessary in order for him to perform the duties incumbent upon the office which he holds. Six months had passed, and Charley had received no call for service while a student in the seminary.

In the summer of 1921, the Baptist state board of Texas and the Baptist Sunday School Board of Nashville, Tennessee, sought seminary students who would go out as summer workers in Sunday school and Training Union enlargement work throughout the associations. Charley was chosen as one of those summer workers. He was accepted for Stephens County Association in Texas.

Stephens County at that time was in a state of a post oil boom. One would need to see a boom city and then behold the desolation following the boom in order to realize the difficulty of the field into which Charley went. Cities had sprung up overnight. If oil were found, the cities grew and remained. If no oil, the places were utterly abandoned. Always, however, the surviving cities settled down to such size and business proportions as the economy of the area made possible. This was a most difficult field for religious workers. Most of the homes were temporary huts. Many of the people who lived in those huts were rich in oil, however. The population consisted mostly of immigrants from all sections of America. Brother Matthews followed the program of the Sunday School Board in taking a religious census and organizing Sunday schools. He was sent as the helper of Rev. T. C. Jordan, a pioneer associational missionary. The two worked together to organize Sunday schools, and in each place preached in a week's revival. They slept where they could find a bed or a cot and ate with the people. Their itinerary lasted three months.

Other dramatic events transpired during that summer. Mrs. Matthews had remained on Seminary Hill with the two children. The little ones were sick much of the time, but faithful Nan never one time called her husband home. It was a real testing time for them both. The pastor of First Baptist Church of Breckenridge,

Texas, Rev. A. J. Morgan, became a very sick man and was confined in a hospital. The church cast about for an interim pastor to supply the pulpit. The lot fell upon the field worker for Sunday school and Training Union, Charley Matthews. From the first day God greatly blessed his preaching, and many people were saved and added to the church during those Sundays he served as interim pastor.

In order to function in this capacity, ordination was necessary and the dreaded hour had come to Charley. He must be ordained in order to baptize converts, serve the Lord's Supper, and perform wedding ceremonies. His membership, along with Mrs. Matthews' and now Byron's, the eldest child, converted at age nine, still remained with the First Baptist Church in Fort Worth. Therefore, Charley came back to Fort Worth to be ordained.

The pastor was away on an extended tour, but the church officials reported to the church the request for Charley's ordination, and prepared for the ordination service. Everything was conducted according to Baptist polity. A Baptist church, after proper examination, through qualified helpers, ordained Charley Everett Matthews to the gospel ministry, in midsummer, 1921. Dr. Matthews returned to Breckenridge and served as interim pastor until Brother Morgan was able to assume his duties again. He had never recovered from the stage fright which embarrassed him from childhood, for every sermon was a battle with Charley Matthews. He trusted in God and did his best.

However, the supreme test of his stage fright was to come when he was asked to perform his first wedding ceremony. The intended groom phoned and asked that the pastor come to a certain address where the wedding was to take place at 8:00 P.M. Charley knew no wedding ceremony and had no church manual from which to learn one. Immediately he went to his faithful missionary friend, Rev. T. C. Jordan. Brother Jordan taught Charley the ceremony which he himself used. He memorized it readily and then Mrs. Jordan suggested that she and Brother Jordan stand together as bride and groom and let Charley rehearse the ceremony with them. He did that at least 20 times.

Following the rehearsal, the Jordans took Charley in their car to the place indicated for the wedding ceremony. A large crowd was gathered under a brush arbor, typical of the oil fields, that was built as a part of a confectionery stand. Charley found the bride and groom and looked at the marriage license.

Already he was trembling from head to foot with anxiety and fear. Stage fright had gripped his entire being and Charley knew that he was predestined to forget that wedding ceremony.

After examining the marriage license, he said softly to the couple, "Move over here in this vacant spot." The Jordans followed. Charley thought he was pulling a fast one with the ceremony, so he asked the couple to join hands by saying, "Because of your choice of each other as partners for life, you will please unite your right hands." They obeyed. Then Charley went blank. Everything left him. He stood there not knowing what to do. Finally he blurted out, "This is a serious business, and you will have to give and take in order to get along." To the groom he asked, "Do you take her to be your wife?" "Yes," he replied. To the bride: "Do you take him to be your husband?" "Yes," she replied. "You are man and wife," he declared. "That is all." And Charley shook hands with them. The crowd milling around began to ask, "When and where are we to have the wedding?" "The wedding is over," said Charley meekly. The Jordans were rolling with laughter and laughed all the way home. Charley never forgot the relief that came to him when he got away from that crowd and his first wedding ceremony.

Charley was embarrassed in that wedding. One other brought chuckles of laughter over the embarrassment of all present. Charley was in bed early one night swathed about his throat and chest with turpentine and woolen cloth. Turpentine was always his favorite home remedy for several ills. Just as he was relaxing amid turpentine fumes, a wedding party walked in downstairs. To get that turpentine off quickly was impossible, he knew. So he grabbed a bottle of high grade perfume, shot some into each hand and plastered it over the turpentine from ears and chin down.

A couple of minutes later he was walking down the stairs, appropriately clad for a wedding ceremony. When he was halfway down the stairs the combination of fumes of turpentine and perfume rose up out of his collar. He said: "There was never anything like that odor. A skunk would have been preferable." Mrs. Matthews and Mary Elizabeth had caught a whiff as he dressed and would not go down. He could not turn back.

He smilingly shook hands all around, hoping his clothing would contain the fumes. By the time he backed up to the fireplace facing the bride and groom with their two attendants, their eyes showed white in shock and consternation. The heat of the fire percolated the odor. Before he could begin he had to say to all present, "Don't be shocked. I brought that odor in here."

He explained what and why it was thus, and the four people facing him began inching backwards to get away. He managed to breathe through it as he hastened the ceremony. By the time he could pronounce the couple man and wife, they were backed against an opposite wall.

Immediately ahead lay another hill which Charley must climb in fiercest battle. Only God could intervene by giving wisdom according to Charley's undergirding Scripture verse, James 1:5. The pastor of the First Baptist Church of Fort Worth had returned home. His former educational director had committed two errors. First, he had enrolled in a school where L. R. Scarborough, who was in the front line of attack by the pastor of the First Baptist Church, was president. The second error lay in the fact that Charley had been ordained by the First Baptist Church in the pastor's absence. Immediately Charley's pastor had his ordination annulled.

Simultaneously the Birdville Baptist Church of the Fort Worth vicinity, second oldest church in the association, had heard Charley with the view of calling him as pastor. Charley had been trapped in the bitter and prolonged fight between the Fundamentalist movement and the Baptist General Convention of Texas. To be pastor of the Birdville Baptist Church he must be a man who was ordained. His only hope lay in securing another ordination.

He remembered that the First Baptist Church granted church letters through the office. Charley therefore phoned the church office and asked that church letters be mailed to him for Byron, Mrs. Matthews, and himself. Following long seasons of prayer and waiting upon the Lord, the voice of God said, "Return to the First Baptist Church of Breckenridge and join there. Have that church ordain you."

Charley caught a train for Breckenridge and found the First Baptist Church in the midst of a great revival meeting under the leadership of Evangelist Charley Taylor and his father. Brother Matthews asked Evangelist Taylor and the pastor to call a conference of the church following the morning service. He then explained to the church how his ordination had been annulled and God had directed him to Breckenridge for ordination. He asked to be received into the church fellowship with letter in hand at the night service, and then to be examined and ordained before adjournment.

Present were sympathizers with the pastor of the Fort Worth First Baptist Church and the Fundamentalist movement. They at once resisted Charley's request, and it seemed for a time that his petition would be denied. Charley declared, "I can preach without an ordination. Dwight L. Moody was never ordained and God blessed him. I can do the same thing and God will bless me." A great Christian layman, C. M. Caldwell, arose and said, "I make a motion that Charley Matthews' request be granted and that we ordain him to the gospel ministry at the close of tonight's service." The motion was seconded and carried without opposition.

Following the night's sermon, September 28, 1921, Charley was examined and ordained by the First Baptist Church of Breckenridge, Texas, in the presence of about 1,500 people. His church letter was granted and placed in his hand, and he headed home, grateful for what God had wrought. Many of those present had been received into the church fellowship during the time that Charley served as interim pastor in Breckenridge. He had a great host of other friends and they have remained true to him through the years.

Charley could now turn his attention to the Birdville Baptist Church, which he accepted as pastor in September, 1921. The church had always been on a part-time basis but began operating full time. In one year the membership jumped from 90 to 180. The church became and remained one of the leading churches in Tarrant County Baptist Association.

While Charley was pastor at Birdville, the Hurst Baptist Church called him to be pastor. He accepted and the church voted to have Sunday school at 2:00 and preaching at 3:00 o'clock, Sunday afternoons. Thus he was pastor of two full-time churches while carrying a full seminary load of 18 hours of classwork.

Within two years of his surrender to God's call to preach, he had completed a year and a half in Southwestern Seminary, and was serving two churches full time. God had wrought one of his miracles in placing his hand upon a man thoroughly dedicated to his will and his work.

VII

Church Expansion and Church Finances

All was going well with the Matthews. The work was being done successfully and the churches were prospering under Charley's ministry. They were looking forward to finishing the seminary, and, thereafter, many years of happy service in the Lord's work, in spite of the 34 years that Charley had lived before he began preaching. But again the Lord had an uphill job for his man from the hills of Missouri. On September 1, 1922, the Travis Avenue Baptist Church of Fort Worth invited Charley Matthews to become its pastor. The church had been constituted in 1910, with 12 charter members, as "South Side Baptist Church." It was renamed "Travis Avenue" in 1921.

God had to work on Charley to get him in the frame of mind to consider the church.

The first person to approach Charley about becoming pastor of Travis Avenue Church was the consecrated associational missionary for whom he had very high regard, the Rev. W. L. Whitley. The two men were standing in the vestibule of the B. H. Carroll Hall on Seminary Hill. Brother Whitley said: "Brother Matthews, Travis Avenue is looking toward you for its pastor." Quick as memory can recall, Charley remembered that he had lived near Travis Avenue during the period before his conversion. He recalled the service he and Mr. Arms had attended there. Travis Avenue, like most other churches in their beginnings, had been in a constant state of more or less strife. There had been so many up and downs and so much strife in the church that some groups had left at one time, and others had split off at other times. The church had become known in the community as "the fighting church."

Charley knew that at one period of such strife, a counsel had been called to advise the young church what to do. Two pastors came and discussed their problem with the church. Both men advised the church to disband. As Charley recalled this bit of unpleasant history in connection with the early days of Travis Avenue, he replied to the missionary's request very quickly, "I don't want to have anything to do with that church. I am satisfied where I am."

But that was not the will of God for the church or for Charley Matthews. The godly Brother Whitley inquired with pain in his voice, "Brother Matthews, won't you at least pray about it?" Charley agreed to pray. He turned and started home. He had not walked a block until God spoke to him. The voice was inaudible, but clearly heard. That changed his mind and his heart. He was humbled by his attitude, and repentant that he should have spoken of any church as he had concerning Travis Avenue. His heart was changed and he wanted to go to Travis. He declared, "It was the most sudden change of mind that I ever experienced."

Before accepting the church, Brother Matthews had a conference with the deacons. That was his first contact in any official way with any group in the church. There were 22 deacons. With a membership of 209, more than a tenth were deacons. Charley said that it appeared to him that half of the men of the church at that time were deacons.

The church presented its plight and whatever challenge there might be in such a situation. It still owned the two lots bought at its organization, 50 by 150 feet, which gave it a total in real estate of 100 by 150 feet. On these lots stood a basement which would seat around 300 persons. Also there was a six-room home for the pastor. The total evaluation of the property was $15,000.00. There was a mortgage against it for $8,000.00. Payments were long past due, and the holder of the mortgage was threatening foreclosure. Sunday school enrollment was 115 and Training Union, about 40. God had spoken to Charley's heart and no circumstances could deter him from accepting the call of the Travis Avenue Church, about three miles from the seminary with few residences between.

The condition of the church was in no wise a reflection on the noble men of God who had served as pastors. There was an attitude in the church that a man's work as pastor would be finished, and then he should move on. A. S. Harwell had stayed two years. Therefore, the church was 12 years old and had had eight men as pastors. In fact, one man showed Charley a hole in Berry Street and said,

"This is where we throw our pastors out on their ears." But Charley found that a great majority of the church members had a real desire to do the will of God as it was revealed to them, they wanted to grow a church. In Charley's own words, "During the years of my ministry as pastor of the Travis Avenue Church, God wrought miracle after miracle in the church. Not all of our undertakings were a success. We experienced failure as well as victory."

However, to the amazement of all, many of the apparent failures turned out to be glorious victories for God in the advancement of his man and that church. As is true in every church, not all the credit is due the pastor for either the failures or the successes. The man is not to be deified in the office of pastor. God must do the work if it is accomplished. On the human side, associated with Charley were competent workers who aided his success, as follows:

Jerry Cox was part-time director of music in 1922 at $50.00 per month. In six months a church secretary was employed at $10.00 per week. At the end of the first year Cox was employed full time. Other men who helped as the years passed were L. L. Cooper, Harry Wootan, Edgar Williamson, B. B. McKinney, Roland Leath, Troupe Reid, Volus Norsworthy, and A. A. Jackson. Paid women workers included Mrs. J. K. Powers, Mrs. Mable Estes, Nannie Lou Williams, Pauline Reid, Ouida Gentry, Frances Holman, Mrs. Jennie Myra Stewart, and Mrs. B. B. McKinney. But there was a constant stream of capable men and women joining the church or being developed in the church so there was ever present outstanding ability and leadership. Thus wrought God, growing a New Testament church.

God wrought miracles in the church fellowship. The truth is sometimes painful, and so this bit is felt. However, if God is to have all the glory from Travis this must be included. In due time the good people in the church who always felt that the pastor had finished his work, began to noise abroad that Charley was through and must move on. It is worthy of note that the same deacon who had shown him the hole in Berry Street where former pastors had landed on their ears, as he jokingly said, was the man who told Charley that the skids were greased for him. The pastor fell again upon his verse, James 1:5. Consternation swept the group who really believed Charley should move, when they arrived for the church conference in which Charley would be notified "in love" that he must go. An overwhelming vote of confidence and pledge to follow the pastor resulted that night. A number of members immediately joined other churches. Others stayed and became party to an unusual "pact of the 26." Those 26 signed a pledge never to critcize or complain without first coming to the pastor and discussing the situation. The pastor immediately signed an identical pledge concerning his behavior toward the 26. The pact remained in the church safe throughout his ministry, and no one ever found reason to call for the application of those terms. The truth is, the tenderest ties developed among all concerned, and their Christian love was so tender and abiding that this is related with hesitancy, for no wound is meant for any. It is history on the negative side which must be included, lest a just criticism be made that only one side of the story was told. It also shows how God wrought. After a period of time the entire membership was adjusted to and respected the leadership of their beloved pastor, Charley Matthews. The achievements in the fellowship of the church and in the increase in membership are phenomenal and miraculous.

Another area in which God wrought miracles was in the finances of the church.

When Charles became pastor, September 1, 1922, the church property was mortgaged for so much that the church could not have liquidated and been out of debt. The church had no credit because of its past-due obligations. But the congregation grew and so did its finances. The Sunday school grew by leaps and bounds, and therein lay the success of growing a congregation, church membership, and a great church budget.

On the first overflow of their house facilities, the elementary departments moved into the parsonage each Sunday. It was very evident that new buildings must be added and equipment arranged for. An emergency existed. The situation was critical.

The only hope for extending the property was to borrow money. The pastor insisted on building for the future. If they could complete the building as originally planned and as was already started, they would have room to seat only 450 people.

An architect was employed. Plans for a new building to seat

1,650 people were adopted. Under the same roof was to be a three-and-a-half story educational building with a swimming pool and a huge gymnasium. In order to construct such a building, it would be necessary for the church to borrow $100,000.00 and to raise an identical amount in one year. For a congregation which could not finish a building to house 450 to launch a program for seating 1,650 persons at an expenditure of $200,000.00 was an unheard-of venture.

Travis was unable, but God was at work. The church prayed without ceasing. There was no hope except in God. And God answered prayer.

One day a stranger came to the pastor's study and introduced himself as Roy Dickey, representing Whitaker and Company, a bond sales company of St. Louis, Missouri. He asked the pastor if he wanted to make a loan for the new building he was planning. The astonished pastor replied, "We certainly do." Mr. Dickey said, "We will loan you $100,000.00 at 6 per cent interest." When the matter was presented to the church, there was such rejoicing as had not been experienced ever by that little congregation. At that time it would have been impossible to find anyone who would believe that a little church with so little to offer as collateral could float a loan of such magnitude. In 1922 there were few churches, regardless of size, which owed as much as $100,000.00.

Just as Charley was facing the staggering task of leading his church through a $200,000.00 building program, he and Dr. George W. Truett of First Baptist Church, Dallas, Texas, were returning from Breckenridge, Texas, where they had conducted funerals of some young people who had drowned. Charley could not see how he could go to school and build that church, and the seminary session would begin in a few days. He, therefore, asked his friend, Dr. Truett, which he should do, drop out of school and build the church or go to school and resign the church.

The wise old pastor said, "Did God call you to the pastorate of Travis Avenue Baptist Church?" Charley said, "Yes."

His friend counseled, "Stay with the church where God has put you. If you cannot attend seminary that should not be fatal to your ministry. Neither did I attend seminary. That realization has made me a diligent student all my life. No, Charley, do not resign the church where God has put you."

Then Dr. Truett continued: "Select carefully the books which you buy. Master them and apply everything to your pastoral work and your pulpit preaching. If you do what God has set you to do, he will take care of the rest." Charley did not enroll in the seminary.

This loan was soon to be pressing like a millstone about the neck of the struggling church. The loan was completed and the church building erected. The congregation moved into the new building early in 1924. Then came the financial struggle.

The church membership was increasing at a rapid rate, but financial obligations were piling up at even greater speed. People were poor. Little money was in circulation. Salaries were at an all-time low. Unemployment was staggering beyond anything in recent years. The church had no pews.

The congregation sat on home-made benches. Someone likened it unto a man with a new suit of clothes who had no shirt or shoes. Through the help of friends and the intervening help of God, Brother Matthews was led to a gentleman by the name of E. O. Edwards, who was persuaded to make an outright gift of $8,000.00 to buy pews. The pews were a memorial in memory of the deceased wife of Mr. Edwards, Sally Ann Edwards. Charley talked with Mr. Edwards many times about his soul, to no avail.

The church was transformed completely with the beautiful golden oak pews, which at this writing could not be purchased for three times the $8,000.00. They are still in use by the church.

However, that did not help make the payments on the mortgage. The bonding company in St. Louis notified the pastor of Travis Avenue Church that three weeks remained before foreclosure proceedings would begin unless $20,000.00 had been remitted during the three weeks. Again the church began to pray without ceasing. Day and night the distressed people cried unto God to provide that $20,000.00 within the three weeks. The church building must be saved.

One week-day morning Pastor Matthews came to the church and found a large group of women on their knees crying to God for help. That morning Charley claimed again his undergirding verse, James 1:5, and sought wisdom from God. Let him tell the story:

I received a profound impression that surely came from the Lord. I carried it out in detail. I went to St. Louis by train to ask Whitaker and Company, our bond holders, then threatening foreclosure, to help to raise the $20,000.00 by making an outright gift of $1,000.00.

Upon arriving at the office, I asked to see the president of Whitaker and Company. I made the appeal of my life. The president listened respectfully but dismissed the whole proposition coldly with a statement of policy: "It has been the established rule of this company since its organization in 1868 never to make a donation to a sectarian cause." I answered, "If your company has set a rule that it will not break, some day that rule will break the company."

The president gazed at the preacher as if in a quandary. Finally he asked, "Did you come all the way from Fort Worth, Texas, to St. Louis to ask me for $1,000.00?" The preacher looked straight into the eyes of his interrogator, and as coozly replied, "I surely did." The president moved in his chair and blurted out, "Well, I will give you $1,000.00 on your gall." He hastily scrawled his signature on the check, and Charley walked out of the office with the $1,000.00 God had sent him to St. Louis to get out of the headquarters of the bonding company. That was a tremendous contribution in that day, and only God could have wrought it.

As Charley stepped into the street, every steam whistle on factories and on boats on the Mississippi River was shrieking; all the bells were ringing; auto horns were blasting; and confetti was falling from windows high above the streets upon the shouting multitudes whose cries intensified the pandemonium. The preacher walked in amazement, wondering how the news of his victory had hit all of St. Louis so quickly, that this expression should be given to a triumphant great-grandson of the Lucas family that helped to found St. Louis. There is always somebody ready to deflate a man and to put another interpretation upon a given situation. After Charles got his head and his hat back to size and properly fitted together, someone shouted, "The St. Louis Cardinals have just won the world series!" Charley joined in the shouting because that victory had come under the leadership of his former baseball teammate in Fort

Worth, Rogers Hornsby, who had led his club to the baseball championship of the world.

No fan of the Cardinals, admiring their championship baseball team, could have been happier than Charley who was championing the finances of the kingdom of God in Fort Worth. No member of the ball club itself could have been more elated than was he over the victory that God had given him. He knew that God had sent him to St. Louis to begin that offering with a gift of $1,000.00 from somebody at Whitaker Bonding Company. He knew that God had wrought in giving him that check for $1,000.00. The company could not do it. The man who gave that check was not in sympathy with what Charley was doing. He had given it to him purely on the basis of Charley's having so much gall. That was before Charley had had a gall bladder operation. He knew that God had sent him $1,000.00 and he was no less elated though the check was delivered by the devil. However, that was just the beginning of thrills in connection with raising that $20,000.00 which had to come forth in three weeks to satisfy the debt.

That night, as Charley headed back to Fort Worth in a Pullman car, he noticed that on the opposite side of the aisle from him sat one of the finest-looking men he had ever seen. This gentleman was tall and handsome, perhaps in his fifties. He was dressed immaculately and bedecked with diamonds on his tie and on his fingers. The Pullman porter brought in a lady and a little boy and set them in the seat that belonged to this fine-looking man's berth. Charley heard the man curse the Negro in his anger for placing someone in the seat that belonged to his berth. Soon most passengers retired to the lounge rooms to prepare for the night while the porter prepared their beds. Charley felt a burden for the soul of this profane man across the aisle from him. Therefore, he sat down by that good-looking stranger and engaged him in conversation.

He informed Charley that he was on his way to Fort Worth to see about some oil wells which he was drilling in Stephens County. Charley had worked in Stephens County, so remarked to this gentleman that he knew something of Stephens County and lived in Fort Worth. The gentleman asked, "Do you know my nephew, Roy Bracewell, who lives in Fort Worth?" "I certainly do," said Charley. "He is one of my dearest friends. I worked with him in the employment of Swift and Company for years." Charley was thrice reinforced for a conversation with this gentleman. First, he was emboldened by getting a check for $1,000.00 in St. Louis. Second, he was emboldened with the consciousness of the presence of God with him. Third, he was a close friend of a nephew of this unusual man. No stage fright hindered Charley now, so he asked, "What is your name?" The gentleman replied, "Jim Blackmon." "Where are you from?" "Chicago," said he. "I live there now and am the campaign manager of Big Jim Kelly, whom we have just elected mayor of Chicago." He explained that he himself had been a mayor for many years in the city of Marion, Illinois.

"Are you a churchman?" Charley asked. "No," he said, "I am not. My father was a Baptist deacon, and my mother was a Sunday school teacher, but I am a black sheep." Charley began witnessing to him about his spiritual needs and read some verses from the New Testament. The man began to perspire and said, "I will visit Travis Avenue Church next Sunday night."

Surely enough, when Sunday night came, there sat Jim Blackmon with a lady friend. At the close of the service the pastor was, as usual, in the baptistry, and did not get to greet Mr. Blackmon. On Tuesday following, Roy Bracewell phoned and said, "Charley, my son Bill is to be married at the bride's home in Arlington Heights on Thursday night. We want you to perform the wedding ceremony. Uncle Jim Blackmon will come by and pick you up and take you to and from the wedding."

At the appointed time Thursday night, Mr. Blackmon stopped a beautiful Cadillac in front of Charley's house, and they were off to the wedding. Any resemblance between that ceremony and Charley's first wedding is purely coincidental. On the way home, Mr. Blackmon pulled the car over to the curb and stopped. He said, "I have to talk with you." Then he began to sob a story that was most unusual. He said, "Last Monday I was driving this car in Stephens County. The woman you saw with me Sunday night was with me in the car. My car suddenly lurched and turned upside down in the ditch. The lady and I were both pinned in the car and neither of us could move. We cried for help as we heard cars passing by, but no one seemed to hear or to see us. Finally I began to pray and I promised God that if he would spare our lives I would give him my heart and my life. Almost momentarily some men stopped and rescued us. Charley, please help me to be saved." Charley spent hours with him until long after midnight, but Mr. Blackmon seemed unable to make a committal of himself to Jesus. He said, "I will be in your church Sunday night."

As the services began Sunday night, there sat Jim Blackmon. When the invitation was given Mr. Blackmon came forward and asked for prayer. Charley said, "Will you please kneel down here while we pray." Then Charley asked for the deacons to come and kneel with the two. During the period of prayer which followed, Mr. Blackmon was gloriously saved, and then was received as a candidate for baptism.

Simultaneously with these miraculous movements that God wrought in this praying church, Mr. C. O. Edwards, who had given the money to buy the pews for the church, and had resisted spiritual appeals, had become interested in his soul's salvation. This multimillionaire philanthropist and ranchman was then 78 years of age. One Sunday morning Mr. Edwards sat in the congregation among the worshippers. His friend, Mr. Dillard, a member, had brought him. When the invitation was given, Mr. Edwards came forward confessing his faith in Christ as his personal Saviour. Charley was shouting happy and later spoke of the incident: "I shall never forget the thrill that came to the hearts of our church members when they heard the name of C. O. Edwards read among those received for baptism."

It was the first time the membership had seen Mr. Edwards. As soon as Mr. Edwards was received the pastor remarked that he would observe the ordinance of baptism following the sermon that night.

Mr. Edwards stood up and said, "I want to go to the crick." Charley explained about the baptistry and all the accommodations needed for the candidate's comfort, and expressed a wish that Mr. Edwards would be baptized in the church. Finally Mr. Edwards agreed to be baptized in the church baptistry provided he could be baptized in the daytime. He followed his Lord in baptism that afternoon.

"With Mr. Blackmon and Mr. Edwards both members of the church, the $20,000.00 was easily raised, and our church building was saved," Charley said. That was the beginning of a series of experiences in paying a church debt that really sounds fantastic and could only be true because God had wrought.

The depression came in 1929. By 1932 the church could not even finance its current obligations. No principal or interest payments could be made upon the mortgaged indebtedness. Many Baptist churches were defaulting on their impossible mortgaged debts.

Travis Avenue kept praying without ceasing for something to happen. The largest income was around $500.00 per Sunday. That would not pay local obligations. To add to the failure of payments on indebtedness or interest, no money could be sent for missions. The nightmare of the depression of the thirties seemed never to end.

The church budget was $4,500.00 per year for missions. Because of the financial hardships, the pastor recommended to the deacons that the church use all receipts to meet local expenses and send no mission money. At that time the pastor began having serious throat trouble. Hoarseness would come upon him in the middle of the sermon. His voice would flicker to almost a whisper. He sought relief from throat specialists in Dallas and in Fort Worth. Every doctor interviewed advised an operation involving his vocal cords. Finally it was decided that Dr. Warwick would perform the operation. Dr. Warwick was reared and educated in Germany. He asked that an X-ray picture be made of Dr. Matthews' throat and head. The pictures were made by Dr. S. R. Hyde and delivered to Dr. Warwick, his neighbor in the Medical Arts Building.

Both physicians advised an operation. The operation was performed. It was very delicate and serious. Nine stitches were taken far down in his throat. Excruciatingly painful soreness and infection followed. Pain was almost unbearable to the patient. On the third day the pastor returned to the doctor for a checkup. Dr. Warwick's flattering remark was, "Your throat looks like something the cats have dragged in." Consultation was called with Dr. Warwick, Dr. Hyde, and the Matthews' family physician, Dr. R. W. McKeon. X-ray pictures were made. The pictures revealed that all of Charley's teeth were diseased and would have to be removed. In addition, the lower right jaw bone, broken by that wagon bed at age ten, was almost eaten in two by infection. The verdict by all three physicians was that the teeth be extracted, the cyst in the jawbone be removed, and a silver plate be placed in the jaw where the cyst was. Brother Matthews said to the physicians, "That means that I can never preach again." They either agreed or expressed little doubt that he had stated the truth.

Charley returned home in such mental suffering that the anguish of his soul seemed more unbearable than the physical pain from infected throat, jawbone, and teeth. He could not eat or sleep. There were no miracle drugs and infection often meant death. Mrs. Matthews went to the corner drugstore to get a prescription filled. The druggist said to her, "Take this *American Magazine* to Brother Matthews. Tell him there are two articles in it that he will be interested in." One article was written by an atheist, the title of which was, "Why I Am an Atheist." The other was written by a Christian, "Why I Am a Christian." Charley read only the article written by the Christian. All he remembers from the article is a Scripture quotation found in Psalm 46:10, "Be still and know that I am God."

Charley testified that he never saw that verse before, or did not remember it. It was like God speaking personally to him. A certain peace came to his mind, the like of which he had never known before. He asked Mrs. Matthews to bring him the Bible. Charley read the same passage from the Book.

As he tried to let that verse master him, he said, "Lord, what have I done to cause this tragedy?" The answer came as plain as day. A voice said, "You are using mission money for other purposes." The answer startled the pastor and gave him a guilty conscience beyond that which he had felt when he had first recommended the action. Anyone who has heard God in an audible voice speak to him knows that at such a time the evil one will thrust in doubts as to its reality.

Charley tested this by saying, "Lord, if you are speaking to me, give me the assurance that this is you. If it is you, heal my throat and I will know that you have spoken." The Lord answered right back, "Why don't you ask me something hard?" Charley was shocked and then said, "Heal my throat and my diseased teeth and jawbone."

71

At that instant the Lord came into his heart with such conscious fullness and peculiar suddenness that the pastor was simply overjoyed, and overwhelmed by the fullness of his presence.

He called Mrs. Matthews and asked that she take him to the doctor's office. On arriving, Dr. Hyde said to Charles, "Sit down, I want to tell you an experience I had." He said, "Night before last I had a dream about you. Last evening my wife and I were at a picture show. I was restless and disinterested. She said to me, 'What is wrong with you? You seem to be disinterested.' I told her that I had had a dream about a preacher the night before and it made me nervous. 'What preacher?' she asked. I said, 'Brother Matthews, pastor of Travis Avenue Baptist Church. I saw a picture of his head, and I could see every bone and it amazed me.'" The doctor continued, "Remove your coat and your shirt. I want to take another X-ray of your head."

When the picture was taken, the doctor said, "Now go to Dr. Warwick and have your throat treated. Then come back here to me." Charley obeyed, and upon returning to Dr. Hyde's office, found that the last picture and the former picture stood side by side. They showed the same head but did not reveal the same condition.

The new picture showed the teeth and the jawbone all to be sound and well. The doctor became excited and sent for Dr. Warwick. Charley rushed to get his family physician, Dr. W. R. McKeon, but he was busy. On his way back, Charley met his friend, a Baptist doctor, L. H. Reeves, a member of Broadway Baptist Church, and asked that he view the pictures. Never can that council of physicians be forgotten.

One of them at that time was an atheist. He spoke first and said that he "could not explain the phenomenon." The other two were Christians. Dr. Reeves said, "Medical science has no explanation for that, only God could have wrought this." Twenty years later, Charley still had all his teeth except one wisdom tooth. He never had any trouble with the jawbone, or suffered hoarseness after that day.

Charley rushed a called meeting of the deacons at the church. He explained his experience. He said to the chairman, J. W. Williams: "Won't you ask the church to vote to make the budget item of missions a preferred item from now on?" That was done and there has never been a month since that Travis Avenue did not send a check for missions. As already stated, the annual amount then was $4,500.00. In 1955, under the leadership of Dr. Robert E. Naylor, Travis Avenue reported more than $60,000.00 given through the Cooperative Program. "God works in mysterious ways his wonders to perform."

The above miracle seems so fantastic that it seems well to let Charley attest it. Here are his words: "I wish to add this to the above experience. I told it from my own pulpit. I related it again and again over the country wherever opportunity afforded. I had in my possession for years the X-ray pictures to show to anyone who doubted the miracle. It is my belief that the redeemed of the Lord should not only give him the credit and the glory for his blessings, but that they should tell the world about them at every available opportunity."

One more miracle as to how God wrought in church finance should be added. In 1936 the depression was at its worst, and the church was at a standstill in attendance and in giving. The budget offerings were $600.00 per week and Sunday school static at 1,000. Two hundred people per year were being baptized and hundreds were being received by letter. However, people were not being enlisted, and the finances had fallen so far behind that the church had no expectancy of ever paying the debt. Hope had vanished. There seemed to be no other way to retain the church property except to find some purchaser for the bonds at a great discount. This was being done all over America by institutions which were settling bonded indebtedness for as little as 25 cents on the dollar. Neither Charley Matthews nor his church members would agree thus to dispose of their obligations in bonded indebtedness.

Again church members turned to prayer unceasingly day and night throughout their waking hours. When God heard them, they were as those who slept. They were like the church praying for the deliverance of Simon Peter from the prison of Herod. They reacted as did the little church when Rhoda answered a knock at the door

73

but hastened back without opening it shouting "Simon Peter is standing at the door." They would not believe it.

The plan revealed to them was that they should get out of their distresses by buying more property, building more buildings, reaching more people, and thereby enlisting more finances. The proposition was presented to the church and passed without a dissenting voice. Two residences were bought and paid for with sacrificial offerings from the people who had been aroused by a new challenge. A steel-and-brick educational building, two stories high, 90 by 140 feet, was soon constructed. A revival preceded the dedication of the new building, and 103 persons united with the church.

Among the congratulatory messages received upon the dedicatory occasion, Charley prized most highly two letters from former teammates of his baseball club. The first was from Sherman Minton, then a member of the United States Senate, and now (1956) a judge in the United States Supreme Court (retired September 7, 1956).

United States Senate
Washington, D. C.
March 3, 1937

Dear Old Matty:

I heartily wish that I might be there on Sunday morning to join with the old gang in doing you honor.

Many years have passed since I was one among you, and all too seldom have I heard from you, but no stretch of time can erase the memories of those days or dim the affectionate regard I have for you and the gang.

With pride and pleasure I have heard from time to time of your success in the ministry, and I am confident of continued success, because you so richly deserve it.

My warmest greetings and best wishes to you and the boys.

Sincerely your friend,
Sherman Minton

The second letter was from Rogers Hornsby, manager of the St. Louis Cardinals, who won the world championship over the New York Yankees. Hornsby is now (1956) in the Baseball Hall of Fame, the greatest right-hand hitter in baseball history. Here's the letter:

Hotel Como
Hot Springs, Arkansas
March 4, 1937
My Dear Rev. Matthews:

I have just learned that you will dedicate an educational building free of debt on Sunday, March 7th, and that some of our old associates will gather at the Travis Avenue Baptist Church to congratulate you. I only wish that I could join them, for your work has made you one of the outstanding ministers of the state of Texas and you are deserving of the highest tribute.

I cannot keep from recalling the old days of association with you in Fort Worth when we played on the local baseball field. My work has taken me far from there, but the lapse of time has not made me forget that you were one of the cleanest and fairest baseball players I ever met. In fact, I have traveled all over the country, meeting the very best in the baseball world, but I have known none fairer than you. This quality is no doubt an aid to you in your chosen field of endeavor and has assisted you to the heights you have attained.

Please remember me to any of the boys with whom I played in the old days, and may I again extend to you my congratulations and best wishes for continued success.

Sincerely yours,
Rogers Hornsby

The week following the revival, six new departments in the Sunday school were organized. These new departments required 84 new workers, all of whom were enlisted in one week. The new building was dedicated free of debt in the spring of 1937. Again God had wrought, and weekly receipts jumped from $600.00 to $900.00 per week.

The additional funds paid off the debt on the church, dollar for dollar, and the budget has continued to grow until now it stands at $7,000.00 per week. All the evidence is that God wrought miracle after miracle in church finances and church expansion.

VIII

Pastoral Evangelism

Charley Matthews' first emphasis throughout the 25 years of his pastoral labors was soul-winning. That was his primary concern. He majored on soul-winning. He gave three reasons for this: first, Jesus came into the world for the one purpose, to seek and to save that which was lost; second, in his commission to his church Christ gave first place to making disciples and baptizing them; third, no Christian can truly follow in the footsteps of Jesus without making soul-winning first in his life.

Dr. Matthews was a firm believer in a pastor's practicing what he preached. If a pastor urges others to win people to Christ, then he himself must be a winner of souls. His close observation through an analytical mind drove him to the conclusion that a soul-winning church could not exist without a soul-winning pastor. His position was that it is just as excusable for a church member to say he is too busy to do personal soul-winning as it is for a pastor, regardless of the size of the church, to say that he is too busy to do personal soul-winning.

Therefore Dr. Matthews, early in his ministry, put aside a day each week to do personal soul-winning. That was a routine that never varied. He continued it throughout his pastoral years. He kept a prospect list of unsaved men, women, boys, and girls in his desk always. Names on the list were made up principally of the unchurched in Sunday school enrollment, and the names of the unsaved men whose wives and children were members of the church. The value of a pastor's doing personal soul-winning regularly each week paid priceless dividends.

Besides winning the lost to Christ, and growing a great church membership, Charley observed that his most effective sermons from Sunday to Sunday were inspired by the experiences he had on the field dealing with sinners. The result was a steady stream of people walking the aisle on Sunday when the pastor extended the invitation. By placing first emphasis upon soul-winning, Charley Matthews saw the church growing at an unusual rate for those years. Dr. E. P. Aldredge, statistician for the Southern Baptist Convention, published the thrilling news that Charley had baptized an average of 173 persons per year during his first 18 years at Travis Avenue. This period covered the years when the church was small and just beginning to grow. During the last five or six years, the average was 200-plus baptisms per year. One year it was 278. That record led in baptisms in the Southern Baptist Convention that year. That was in the middle thirties, when the church was experiencing great financial struggle. Of course many churches now baptize 200, but in those days that was an unusual record. When Dr. Matthews resigned Travis Avenue Church, the membership stood at 6,034, which was 727 more souls than Spurgeon's church membership at its peak, the time of Spurgeon's death, 1892: "Spurgeon's membership was 5,037."* Charley's membership could never have been built without first-place emphasis upon soul-winning.

Every conversion is a miracle of God and is worthy to be told many times over. Only a few outstanding conversions are being related here to encourage other soul-winners, for God wrought at Travis Avenue through pastoral evangelism.

The salvation of one person is as precious and as miraculous in the plan of God as is the salvation of any other. However, four conversion experiences are given because of unusual events surrounding them. All showed definitely how God wrought. They are related for God's glory.

Three of these conversion experiences are of men of affairs, one a precious girl, age seven. As a rule it is much easier to win a down and out, than it is to win an up and out to Christ. These three men were in the circles of worldly success but were out of the kingdom of God.

A nephew of President Wm. A. McKinley, born to a sister of President McKinley, was A. J. Duncan, president of the Texas

*The Shadow of the Broad Brim, page 99; The Judson Press. Used by permission.

Electric Service Company, of Ft. Worth, Texas. But as Naaman, the Syrian, was a leper, Mr. Duncan was an unbeliever. The first time Pastor Matthews called upon Mr. Duncan, he was courteous and easy to talk with. He was a well-educated man and one of the greatest engineers of the area. But when the pastor mentioned Christ to him, he exploded with, "I do not believe that Christ is any more divine than you are divine. To say that a man died on the cross 2,000 years ago and that the blood he shed at his death has anything to do with me, is preposterous." He was simply too difficult for the pastor to impress. Let him rest.

The conversion that probably influenced Charley Matthews' ministry more than any other was one in which he did not have a leading role. It was the conversion of his first-born daughter, the second child, Kathryn Louise. The family was living on Seminary Hill and he was pastor at Birdville in 1922. Kathryn was seven years old. She was under conviction of sin. It was about 8:30 Sunday morning and the family was preparing to leave for Birdville. She went into the room where her mother was and began asking her questions about how to be saved. Mrs. Matthews opened her Bible and read to Kathryn, explaining the way of salvation as she went along. The story is better told in Charley's own words for this volume:

I looked at them and they were on their knees praying. Presently Kathryn came running to me laughing through her tears. She said, "Daddy, I have trusted Jesus and he saved me."

From that day forward Kathryn loved religious activities, I believe, to a greater degree than any child I have ever known. She was very talented. She could sing, play the piano, and speak unusually well before a congregation. She loved parts in the drama that was regularly staged by the children in the church. Just a few days before her death she was in a religious play. She played the part of an angel. Her costume included huge white wings. We kept that costume for years. She unbelievably could teach a Sunday school lesson to children as efficiently as an adult.

Her Sunday school teacher in the Junior Department was in poor health, and was absent much of the time. Kathryn happily seized upon the opportunity to teach the lesson as supply for ten-year pupils. Always it was upon the insistence of the class and the consent of the department superintendent. She had a neighborhood group of children numbering around 20, whom she would assemble in the shade of the parsonage regularly in the summertime. She would keep them for hours singing children's hymns and telling Bible stories. One of her converts is Wayman Whitley, pastor at Bisby, Texas, as this is written.

We did not know of her soul-winning until her body lay in state in our home. Mrs. Matthews was worn from four days of vigil at Kathryn's bedside in the hospital, and was prostrated with grief. The house was crowded with friends, and members of the church. I asked Mrs. Matthews, "Mother, whom do you desire to act as pallbearers for Kathryn?" She answered, "Her Sunday school class members." And Mrs. John Blaylock spoke up and said, "Kathryn won my Frances to Christ." Two other mothers followed in saying, "Kathryn led my girl to Christ, too." I do not remember their names. All three of the children were members of Kathryn's class and were pallbearers.

Her classroom was memorialized by her department. The name, "The Kathryn Class" was painted over the class door and the room was decorated suitably with Kathryn's pictures in it. Another use of this dedicated room was for prayer. The room remained as a memorial for 30 years, having been changed recently when the educational building was redecorated.

At Kathryn's funeral, the house seating some 1,600 was full to capacity. Dr. Scarborough and Dr. Jeff D. Ray conducted the funeral. Dr. Scarborough said to me at the cemetery, "Charley, this is the largest funeral for a child that I have ever witnessed." Not only was the church membership shocked and affected by Kathryn's going, but church attendance at that time greatly increased. Other churches likely were affected by Kathryn's deathbed experience.

Kathryn's deathbed experience changed her parents. They were never the same any more. Personally, I never doubted that Christ is alive, but Kathryn saw him and recognized him as he opened the door for her. It was such a vivid revelation to her and so definitely clear to us as a reality, that we could never doubt Christ's existence any more than Saul of Tarsus could after he talked with Jesus and said, "Who art thou, Lord?"

The broken heart of Charley Matthews had become a new power-house for the living Lord Jesus Christ. From that day on there was a new cry in his soul for lost men and a greater response on the part of individuals and the multitudes, to trust the Christ of Kathryn and her family.

The Ft. Worth *Star Telegram* picked up the story of Kathryn's death in the Baptist hospital and gave front-page feature stories to her experience and also to her funeral. The experiences of the Matthews family became a topic of conversation and lament in households as far as the circulation of the Star Telegram reached. None will ever know the outreach of that influence. It is best illustrated in the story of another conversion.

About two weeks after her going, Dr. Matthews was at the cashier's window paying his light bill in the Texas Electric Service Company Building. Mr. Duncan saw him and came and asked that he come to his office. When the two were seated in the president's private office, Mr. Duncan turned to the pastor, whose appeal he had spurned so recently, and asked that he tell him the story in detail, relative to the homegoing of his little daughter. When Brother Matthews finished the story, Mr. Duncan without any persuasion was gloriously saved. He was the one who spearheaded the drive and made possible the construction of the educational building of the Travis Avenue Church during the depression in 1937. Mr. Duncan also gave a large sum of money to the Baptist Hospital of Ft. Worth. He helped Southwestern Seminary numbers of times over a period of years. He was a man of wealth and unusually generous.

Another outstanding conversion in Travis Avenue was that of Mr. L. L. Winans. Mrs. Winans was an unusually talented musician and for years was the leader of the church orchestra. She had four children, three daughters and a son. The mother was received by letter and the four children were converted and baptized into the fellowship of Travis Avenue Baptist Church.

The husband and father was not a believer. He was a well-educated man and a great engineer in the employment of the United States Government. Dr. Matthews and other men of the church visited him in the interest of his salvation. Mrs. Winans and the children became so greatly burdened by their father that they cried out in their distress for the help of their church. Many of the church members joined the pastor and the family in prayer that Mr. Winans might be saved.

Dr. Matthews made another call with the hope that some interest on the part of Mr. Winans might be manifest. He met with almost scoffing dissent. Mr. Winans said, "I do not any more believe that

Christ's death meant any more to this world than the death of any other person. I think the idea of Christ's shedding his blood for sinners is silly." Then he asked, "Do you have a Greek New Testament?" Dr. Matthews replied that he did not, but the same day he bought one and presented it to Mr. Winans.

The next Sunday at the 11:00 o'clock worship hour, Dr. Matthews saw to his great surprise that L. L. Winans was sitting with his family in the congregation. It was the first time the pastor could remember seeing him inside the church. When the invitation was given, Mr. Winans came forward, publicly confessing his faith in Christ as Saviour, and forthwith was baptized. Dr. Matthews said that Mr. Winans grew in the Word of God and in grace faster than any person he observed throughout his ministry.

In only a few weeks, Mr. Winans was teaching a class of young men in the Sunday school. That was about the year 1939. Today, 1956, Mr. and Mrs. Winans are stationed on the island of Guam. There he has charge of one of the departments of the United States Government. Better still, Mr. and Mrs. Winans are operating a mission on the island and carrying on an intensified program there for Christ.

The leading of Col. E. E. Dickie, at that time president of the Williamson, Dickie Garment Manufacturing Company, second largest of its kind in the world, will never be forgotten as long as members of Travis Avenue live. Mr. Dickie was president of the company that makes work clothes for men. They are sold throughout America. Mr. Dickie's name was secured by a census taker in preparing for a revival. Dr. and Mrs. Matthews were handed the census card by Mrs. Avinger. She said, "Mr. Dickie asked that the pastor call by his home." Dr. Matthews made the call on Saturday afternoon. It was the first time he had met Mr. Dickie.

As they sat in the living room of the Dickie mansion, the pastor said, "I came here at your invitation, and am happy to be of any assistance possible to you." Mr. Dickie said, "Let me tell you briefly about myself. I started making my own living at the age of 14, as a dishwasher in a restaurant in Waco, Texas. I am a very selfish person. I have devoted my life to making money. In that I have succeeded. I have been too selfish even to get married. I did look

81

after my mother until her death. And my only sister lives with me now. She is on her deathbed.

"About two months ago I buried my own brother. At the cemetery I sat in a chair beside his open grave. As his casket was lowered into the grave I thought I heard someone say, 'E. E. Dickie, you are the greatest failure in this world. You are 68 years of age and have devoted all your time and energy to making money. Soon you will be lowered into the grave like your brother, and you are unprepared to meet God.' Preacher, I want you to tell me how to prepare to meet God."

The preacher read to him the story of Philip and the Ethiopian eunuch, as found in Acts, Chapter 8. Then he asked Mr. Dickie if he could put to him a few simple questions. He replied, "Sure." The pastor said, "Do you believe there is a supreme being?" "Yes," he answered, "I do." "Do you believe the Bible is God's Word?" "I do," he said. Then he asked if he believed that Jesus is God's Son, and that he died for our sins. "I do," he said. Then he said, "Mr. Dickie, do you believe it strongly enough that you are willing to trust Jesus as your Saviour and risk the destiny of your soul now, on your deathbed, and after that throughout an endless eternity in his hands?" The rich man stared at the preacher for a moment and said, "I would have to know more about him before I would risk my destiny in his hands." At such an instant Charley Matthews always prayed. Therefore, he said, "Let us pray." They both knelt and prayed.

It was the pastor's intention to ask Mr. Dickie to pray, but he arose to his feet too soon. The pastor asked him again, "Are you now ready to trust Jesus to save you?" He said, "I will be in your church tomorrow." His was no idle promise as is made in similar circumstances by so many people, in order to dodge the issue. A revival was in progress, with Wade Freeman of First Baptist Church, Sulphur Springs, Texas, preaching. The next morning there sat Mr. Dickie in front of the preacher when he arose to preach. When the invitation was given, many came forward making their decisions. But Mr. Dickie did not move. The pastor walked back to where he stood and said to him, "Mr. Dickie, God has spoken to you again. Won't you trust Jesus now to save you?" He answered, "Let me think it over." The pastor said, "You have had 68 years to think it over. Isn't that time enough?" A man was present who was employed by Mr. Dickie's firm. He came up and said, "Colonel, you had better do what the preacher said, for he is right." Mr. Dickie said to the pastor, "Will you walk with me to the front?" The two came forward and Mr. Dickie took his stand for Christ.

That was one of those dramatic hours in the history of Travis Avenue when God walked in the midst of the congregation in his temple. There were more than 60 who had come forward and they were presented to the congregation by name. Mr. Dickie stood among the others. He was a large man, tall, and weighed around 250 pounds. Such a contrast is seldom seen as this big man stood next to a little Junior girl who had come forward to make her decision for Christ also. God has no limits of size or age for salvation. The congregation was electrified, and the house was filled with the Shekinah glory.

The pastor said, "Mr. Dickie, have you trusted Jesus to save your soul this morning?" He answered, "I have." "Are you satisfied that he has saved you?" "Yes, I am." "Do you want to be baptized in our church?" "Yes, I do." When the church had received those whose names were read, the pastor announced that he would observe the ordinance of baptism that evening.

Mr. Dickie stood at that moment and asked to be baptized now. He had continued to read the story of Philip and the eunuch after the pastor left his house the day before. He had noticed how insistent the eunuch was upon being baptized, and that Philip baptized him as soon as he said that he believed that Jesus Christ was the Son of God. Mr. Dickie refused to leave the building until he was baptized.

Mr. Dickie was genuinely converted. One of his first acts was to make a very liberal gift to Southwestern Seminary. He became a faithful church member and soul-winner.

No doubt the most striking experience which the pastor had in making one call and baptizing five young men as a result came to him at Travis. And that victory, as did so many others, came from apparent failure. It was the first Sunday night of the New Year, and the pastor had been inspired by reading a sermon by Dr.

George W. Truett about the words, "Lot lingered." The pastor wrote out his sermon, and then preached it with a feeling of genuine liberty. When the invitation was given, not a person moved. The pastor was heartbroken for there were large numbers of unsaved people in the audience. He left the service feeling that he had completely failed, and spent a sleepless night fretting about his failure.

The next day a young man phoned him and asked that he come to his apartment where he and some friends wanted to talk with him about a religious problem. The pastor reached the apartment about 7:30 P.M.

There were five young men who were all employees of the First National Bank of Ft. Worth, Texas. The one who had phoned him was named Paul Hamilton. He said, "Brother Matthews, we were all five in your service last night at Travis Avenue. None of us is a member of any church. When you gave the invitation for people to accept Christ, I had a strange feeling come over me. I did not go forward, but I believe that I trusted Christ then for I am very happy and have unusual peace of mind." The pastor asked, "Is that the first time you have ever felt as you do?" He replied, "It is."

Then one by one all five men said, "I had the same experience as Paul did last night and am ready to join the church." All five were baptized the next Sunday and all five still are employed by the First National Bank of Ft. Worth. Paul Hamilton is one of the vice-presidents of the bank.

Those who heard the lamented George W. Truett preach, or read his books, never think of him without thinking of the conversion of Big Jim. It was related countless times in as many places by the great pastor of the First Baptist Church of Dallas. It was publicized in his writings. It was magnified in the *Baptist Standard* in an article written by Dr. J. B. Gambrell under the caption, "The Greatest Conversion I Ever Witnessed." In one of the cattlemen's revivals which Dr. Truett conducted each year, two men claimed the promise of Jesus in Matthew 18:19. As Dr. Truett walked he overheard two men claiming that promise, the preacher's text, for Big Jim. When Big Jim was saved those rugged ranchmen nearly tore up the ranch in their great joy. Because of Jim's previous life his conversion was long a topic of conversation, and an illustration for many a sermon.

One night when Charley stood in his pulpit to preach, four strangers sat in the congregation. They were two men and two women, two couples. Charley had never seen them before. In the invitation, all four came forward. One lady came on the promise of letter, and the other lady and both men came for baptism.

On the next Sunday night, when they were preparing for the baptismal service, one of those men handed the pastor a clipping from the *Baptist Standard*. It was 25 years old, and bore the headline, "The Greatest Conversion I Ever Witnessed." Dr. Matthews quickly asked, "Are you related to Big Jim?" He answered, "I am his son, and the lady that came by letter is his daughter, my sister." Therefore, Charley baptized the son of Big Jim, his wife, and the husband of his sister, Big Jim's daughter. They made excellent church members.

But along with evangelism on the part of the pastor, he helped a large number of young people to give their lives in full-time religious service as soul-winners. One of the outstanding blessings that came to the ministry of Charley Matthews during his long pastorate at Travis Avenue was the large number of young people who surrendered to special service. There were more than 50 of those young people and most of them were baptized at the hands of Charley Matthews, their pastor. It is dangerous to name any of them lest others might feel slighted. The records reveal that some of them are oustanding in the service of Christ today. It is wished that all of them could be named and their records given. That is impossible.

Not named elsewhere, here are a few: Dr. W. Fred Swank, for 21 years pastor of Sagamore Hill Baptist Church of Ft. Worth, Texas. Dr. Swank has led that church from a membership of 200 with practically no property under a roof that leaked like a sieve, to a membership of 4,000, and property valued at $1,000,000.00. Others are Dr. William Shamburger, pastor of the First Baptist Church of Tyler, Texas; Dr. Otis Strickland, president of Decatur Baptist Church; Dr. Paul Brooks Leath, pastor of the First Southern Baptist Church, Fresno, California; Dr. Joel Ferguson, foreign missionary to Nigeria; Kathryn Cozens, the great Brazilian missionary stationed in Recife, Brazil; Rev. Gene McKinney, son of B. B., professor in Baylor University; Dr. Wiley Osbourne, Ph.D., professor in Wake Forest College; Mrs. Rogers Smith, whose husband is on the administrative staff of the Foreign Mission Board; Mrs. Glenn Crotts, wife of the pastor of the First Southern Baptist Church, Tucson, Arizona; and a host of others.

Almost all of these surrendered for special service during the annual Travis Avenue Youth Encampment, Camp Travis, conducted for 21 successive years during Dr. Matthews' ministry. He said the encampment was the highlight in the ministry of that church. Young people who were saved during camp and answered the call to special service are preaching the gospel in many places throughout the world.

Thus God wrought through pastoral evangelism.

IX

Revival Meetings

Charley Matthews also believed that pastoral evangelism included the conducting of at least one revival each year in the church by the pastor himself. Also the pastor should be an evangelist in as many revival meetings in other churches as his schedule will permit.

Dr. Matthews conducted 23 revivals in Travis Avenue Baptist Church in the 24 years he was pastor, and one revival five years after he resigned. But Charley had to be converted to the idea that a pastor should preach revivals in his own church. Let him tell it:

I had an idea that possesses many pastors as follows: first, the people want to hear a new voice; second, I would have to preach new sermons; and third, the people would not come to hear me.

The third year at Travis, some of our consecrated young people emerged from a prayer meeting. It was on an afternoon in August. They came to me with a request. The spokesman was Miss Lois Hall, now wife of Roland Leath, at this writing minister of music and education in First Baptist Church, Shelby, North Carolina. She began by asking, "Pastor, when are we going to have our revival?" "In the fall sometime," I replied. "Why wait until next fall?" she replied. "We will be away in college then. We want a revival now." 'Well, I do, too, but we can't get the preacher we want until October," I said. She stared at me and finally said, "Didn't God call you to preach?" "Yes, he did," I answered. "Then why don't you preach?" she asked. I enquired, "When do you young people want this revival?" "Right now, beginning next Sunday," she said.

I phoned the Dallas Tent and Awning Company and secured a tent, 60-by-120 feet. Then I phoned B. B. McKinney at Southwestern Seminary and asked if he could lead our music. Brother McKinney could help us, so we had secured the tent and the singer. I was fearful and trembling, because my first and only revival in Travis Avenue Church had been begun two weeks after I was called as pastor. Then the church was small, I was new, and there were few prospects, but we had 54 additions.

This request for revival was more than two years later and we had more people. We began the revival meeting on the following Sunday and continued two weeks. There were 174 additions with more than 100 by baptism. That group of young people petitioned me to use my old sermons. I did, and I am still preaching them in revivals."

From that time the pastor did the preaching in from one to two revivals each year. Some of these revivals were near pentecostal experiences. There were more than 100 additions to the church in every one of them. When asked what was the ruling element from the human standpoint in these revivals, the pastor replied quickly, "Two things, prayer and visitation."

Revivals in other churches made up a vital portion of the ministry of Charley Matthews. His first revival was in his home community in Missouri in August, 1922. That was one month before he became pastor of Travis Avenue. He was a student in Southwestern Seminary.

The place of the revival was the little town of Red Bird, Missouri. None of his people had heard him preach, nor had they seen him since he had surrendered to the ministry. He had with him J. Campbell Wray, a student then in Howard Payne College at Brownwood, Texas. Wray had charge of the music. He was the same Wray who later became head of the School of Music in Southwestern Seminary in Fort Worth, and is at this writing in the School of Music in Mary Hardin Baylor College, Belton, Texas.

Matthews and Wray arrived at the old home community on Sunday morning. That afternoon they went to the home of Brother Matthews' grandmother, Mrs. P. J. Lacy. It was like the meeting in the home of Cornelius. A gathering of relatives and friends numbering 65 had assembled at the home. Mrs. Lacy was the mother of Dr. Matthews' mother. She asked that they have services in the yard.

Campbell Wray played a number on his trumpet and led the group in a song. Then Brother Matthews read from the book of John, Chapter 3, and started preaching a sermon which was never finished. He remembered the many letters which he had written to his grandmother since his conversion, and how that in each letter he had urged her to consider Christ as her Saviour. She had always returned loving replies without any reference to Christ.

As he stood in that yard in that farm house on the apex of a Missouri hill, his concern for his grandmother was so great that he had difficulty holding back the tears. He asked, "Grandma, do you believe what I have read?" She answered, "Course I do." Then she said, "Charley, will you baptize me?" "Yes, I will if you have trusted in Jesus to save you." She answered, "I have." Dr. Matthews later said, "That was the greatest thrill of my ministry."

Charley preached as best he could and extended the invitation. That night he preached in a church at Red Bird. When he gave the invitation, the first to come forward to accept Christ as Saviour was his oldest sister, Mrs. W. E. Gorman. The second one to respond was her daughter, his niece, now Mrs. Esther Milner, the chairman of the deaconesses in the Third Baptist Church in St. Louis, Missouri. She is following in the steps of her godly mother, who was for years a deaconess in the same church. Mrs. Milner is a noted gospel singer, having for years been a member of the famous quartet in the Third Baptist Church, of which Dr. C. Oscar Johnson is pastor. And the youngest son of his deceased mother, Floyd, the baby that she had asked to kiss as she was dying, gave his heart to Christ that night, as did his wife.

At the conclusion of this first revival in Missouri, Dr. Matthews baptized 45 persons in the Burbois River, the beautiful Ozark Mountain stream near Red Bird. The most of the 45 who were baptized were his relatives, and all were received into nearby Baptist churches.

The next year Dr. Matthews returned to his home community for another revival. At that time he preached at Highgate Baptist Church. The number of additions in this revival was exactly the same as in the first one at Red Bird the previous year, 74. This time he baptized 52 in the Burbois River. Just as the conversion of his grandmother was the red letter incident in his first revival, the conversion of his two other brothers in the second revival marked the high point. Those brothers were then grown men and prominent citizens in Shannon County. They hired a man to bring them in a Model T to hear their brother from Texas preach. Charley preached that first Sunday morning with the brothers present, but they did not respond. That afternoon their chauffeur began talking about something being wrong with the car. He proceeded to tear it apart and arrange it in little piles around under a tree. He did not go to church that night but was out there tinkering with the car. When Charley came in from the preaching service, he looked up and asked, "What happened?" Charley replied, "They did not respond." The man bowed his head and began fingering automobile parts again. He was a short, squatty hillbilly, with a handle-bar mustache that could be tied behind his neck. In contrast, he had only a fringe of hair.

Monday morning they had to get back to attend to the farms, the cattle, and their business interests. But the car was torn down, not ready. That afternoon Charley's brothers were rather unhappy, and said, "If that car won't run in the morning we are going home on the train." So they heard Charley preach again that night. Crowds came on foot, horseback, and in wagon loads from every direction. The power of God had been mightily felt in every service. Monday night when Charley gave the invitation, he saw Champ lean his head on the shoulder of his brother, Warren, and start sobbing. Before Charley could get back to them, arm in arm they staggered down into the aisle and came forward trusting the wonderful Saviour who had done so much for Charley and whom Charley was now offering to them. With them came Mary, the wife of Champ. They were the last members of Charley's family to be saved. They were baptized and have made marvelous Christian men.

That night when Charley reached the man who was tinkering with the car, again he asked Charley, "What happened?" "They were both saved," Charley said. "Goody! Then I can put the car together and we can go." The astonished Charley said, "Wasn't there anything wrong with this car?" The evangelistic reply was, "Course not."

On Tuesday and thereafter day services were conducted. The church building would not hold the crowds. Charley preached to them from the back of a Ford truck.

In the meetings which Dr. Matthews conducted in his boyhood community, in St. Louis and East St. Louis, 79 of his relatives were saved and added to the churches.

What Dr. Matthews regarded as the greatest revival he ever conducted was the one in the First Baptist Church of Erick, Oklahoma, in 1927. The full impact of the glorious home-going of his precious daughter, Kathryn, together with the constant companionship and transforming power of his risen, reigning Lord, had transformed Charley Matthews from a timid man, harassed by stage fright, into a flaming evangelist, brave as a lion. The song leader for the great revival in Erick was Jerry Cox, at this writing pastor at Foyil, Oklahoma. The meeting was conducted under and around a tent that had been used previously as a skating rink.

The tent was pitched by the side of the church building. So great was the crowd that only a small portion of the audience could be seated under the tent. The preacher declared that he had never seen such spiritual power in all his life. There was nothing like it before nor exactly like it afterwards. Just a few people had prayed for a revival. One old saint, a Confederate veteran by the name of White, had prayed for years that God would permit him to live to see the wicked saved.

On the other hand, there was a retired ranchman in the town who was a vile atheist. This man had quite a following. He would sit throughout the day in front of a store, chewing tobacco and whittling as he preached his atheism. One of his followers was the orchestra leader who played for the dances previously conducted under the tent. The pastor told Charley that the atheist would attend only one service in a revival and would then assemble his followers on the next day at the town meeting place and pick the evangelist's sermon to pieces. The pastor was B. A. Ethridge, and Erick is located on Highway 66, nicknamed "The main street of North America."

Charley's first sermon was delivered on Monday night. The orchestra leader sat with the choir and sang. Thirty-four people responded to the invitation at the conclusion of the message. Most of these were adults coming by profession of faith. It made a profound impression upon the orchestra leader.

The next night the atheist attended. When the invitation was given, 42 persons made professions of faith in Christ, among them the orchestra leader. After the service, the orchestra leader walked home with the atheist. He said, "Dad, you are wrong. There is a God and Jesus Christ is his son, for I trusted him tonight and he saved me. I am so happy I do not know how to express it."

The next night the atheist came again. The congregation seemed to sense the fact that old "Dad" Roberts was under conviction that night. Undoubtedly hundreds were praying that God would convict him.

"Dad" Roberts was a big man. He wore a heavy mustache and made a very imposing appearance. Yet people seemed to dread his appearance, he was so bold and well read in matters pertaining to religion. He was known throughout western Oklahoma as an enemy of Christ and his church. For years he had spread his heresy with almost unbelievable destructiveness among the people, old and young. He was a veritable thorn in the flesh of churches in that section of the state. But the Holy Spirit is mighty too, in his convicting power, and when the invitation was given, Dad Roberts started to the front. The greatest demonstration of joy ever beheld in a revival meeting conducted by Charley Matthews broke loose at that instant. All eyes seemed at once to look upon God when he started to the front. People actually threw their arms about each other, some weeping, some laughing with joy, and others, throwing their hats in the air, shouted. People were seated in rows covering an acre of ground outside the tent. When standing, they were under trees, and their hats could be seen as they sailed up in the limbs of the trees as the people shouted. Dad Roberts, the atheist, had come to God.

When he arrived at the altar, the preacher asked, "Are you trusting Christ to save you?" He said, "My God! pray for me." The two knelt and the people sang and shouted. Charley prayed. Surely Dad prayed, too, for the noise was so great that the preacher could scarcely hear his own voice. Presently Dad cried out, "It is settled. It is settled! God has forgiven me. Oh, I am so happy!" Every night thereafter, for the remainder of the two weeks, from 30 to 60 people were saved and hundreds dedicated their lives in service for Christ.

One night, a family, consisting of a mother and four children, came forward to accept Christ as Saviour. The preacher asked, "Do you want to unite with the church and be baptized?" The lady explained that they were leaving early in the morning for California. They were on vacation. Their home was in New Jersey. The woman said, "We stopped at a motel down the road about sundown. We saw people passing in cars and wagons and wondered where they were going. All of a sudden a strange feeling came over us and we did not know what caused it. We felt as though something was pulling us, something fastened to us on the inside. Now I know what it was. It was God's power. We just came along and surely we shall join the church when we return home."

At one of the morning services starting at 10:00 o'clock, a large number came forward publicly confessing their faith in Christ as Saviour. One was the owner of a lumber yard. He was a nice-looking man about 50 years of age. He asked that he might say something. The preacher relied, "Certainly." He said, "I have been a wicked man and am not fit to come here to this revival." A lady in the congregation who was a next-door neighbor and friend arose and interrupted him by saying, "I am that man's next-door neighbor. He is a good man and a good citizen." The man cut her off short as he turned to say to her, "Sister, will you please sit down and let me do my own repenting."

In another morning service, the preacher was interrupted when a man came running into the tent. He did not stop but kept running right down the aisle. Charley did not know what was wrong with him. He yelled to the preacher, "Stop! Stop! I want to say something." Charley said, "All right, say what you want to." He said, "I was waiting on customers over there in my grocery store. Something got hold of me. I don't know how to describe it. I felt that if I did not come over here and confess my sins I would die. I just left the customers at the store and ran over here." He looked up at the preacher and said, "Preacher, I acknowledge Christ as my Saviour. Pray for me." The service was turned into a prayer meeting as they knelt to pray for this man. He prayed aloud. He did not ask God to save him; he thanked God for having saved him. When he had finished his prayer, he said, "It is all right with me and God. Thank everybody." He went back to the store after he was received for baptism. Charley said, "As long as I live I shall never get away from that Erick revival."

It is estimated that 1,000 persons made decisions of some kind, in a town of 2,000 people. Out of that group 379 were added to the church at Erick. Of this number 251 came for baptism. There were three baptismal services, 191 being baptized in a lake on the last

Sunday afternoon. There were only 300 members in the church when the revival started, so the membership had more than doubled!

However, 1928 was to bring to Charley Matthews the most glorious revival he ever witnessed inside a church building. It was in the First Baptist Church of Electra, Texas, a city of some 4,000 people. Rev. W. W. Rivers was the pastor. In that revival, there were 298 additions to the church, around 250 for baptism. It was a revival of power such as one seldom experiences in a lifetime.

The reason for such outpouring of the Spirit of God in this revival remains a mystery. The usual preparation was made such as the prayer meetings and publicity. A normal amount of visitation was carried on during the progress of the revival. The power of the Holy Spirit gripped the hearts of the church members and non-members alike.

The Spirit's presence was evident over a radius of ten miles. Every service was marked with some special demonstration of God's power. For instance, in the closing service, some 50 persons united with the church. One man came forward to confess his faith in Christ as Saviour. Charley asked him, "What is your age?" He replied, "Sixty-eight." Then a truly aged man came forward on confession of faith. The two threw their arms about each other, both of them weeping with unbounded joy. Charley asked, "Are you two men related?" The 68-year-old man said, "Yes, he is my father." "How old are you?" Charley asked, and the father replied through his tears, "I am 88."

Another never-to-be-forgotten revival took place in Hubbard City, Texas, the First Baptist Church, where the Rev. M. O. Cheek was pastor. That was the home town of Tris Speaker, manager of the Cleveland Indians, one of whose teams Charley pitched against in Fort Worth some years before.

Services were conducted under a tabernacle which was used for revivals for all denominations, county fairs, and other community assemblies. The meeting started slowly with average crowds and average interest. At the beginning of the second week a real revival broke out. Throngs of people were affected and scores were being saved in every evening service. One night a man came from far out away from the tabernacle. Charley met him at the altar. As they

94

clasped hands, Charley felt the man's hands quivering, and noticed that he was trembling from head to foot, like a leaf in the wind. They prayed and this man made a public confession of faith in Christ, along with some 20 others, and they were approved for baptism. The great crowd lingered after service for some 30 minutes.

After the service closed, a Mr. Jim Weatherby, president of the bank, came to Charley and said, "Brother Matthews, I will never doubt God again." "Why is that?" He said, "The wickedest person, save one, I have ever known was saved tonight. The person who is wickeder is the man's wife." He was referring to the man who came under such conviction that he was trembling so that he could hardly stand.

The bank president then explained to the preacher that the couple lived on a large farm outside the city, that their farmhouse was a bootlegging joint, a bawdy house, and a gambling center. The wife was living with her fifth husband. She even controlled the politics in the county, he said. The woman's name was on the lips of the people over the county. She was called Kate, and had lacked only a few hours of graduating from Baylor University, where she was a classmate of the famous W. T. Conner, of the Southwestern Seminary faculty.

The next night a large number of automobiles with people seated in them surrounded the tabernacle. When the invitation was given, men and women were coming from all the cars making decisions for Christ. Charley noticed a woman getting out of a car parked just outside of the tabernacle. She came to the front. She was large, well groomed, and attractive. She extended her hands and stood there speechless. Finally Charley said, "What is it you wish to do?" She said, "Will God have mercy on the meanest person on earth?" He answered, "Though your sins be as scarlet, he will make them white as snow." She asked, "Would you pray for me?" The two stood there with her praying to God for mercy on her soul. The music drowned out the preacher's voice. At the conclusion of the prayer he asked, "Are you now ready to trust Christ as your Saviour?" She said, "I am."

News of Kate's conversion spread over that section of the state like wildfire. The pastor baptized the new converts on Sunday afternoon. The church house, a large building seating around 1,000 persons, was filled to overflowing. It was the opinion of the church leaders that the multitudes had come to see Kate baptized. As she stood with the pastor in the baptismal waters, a hush came over the congregation. As Brother Cheek repeated the baptismal formula and baptized Kate, there seemed to be a blanket of white covering the audience. The flash of white was the hundreds of handkerchiefs raised to the faces of the people as they wiped tears from their eyes.

Charley returned two years later for another revival at the First Baptist Church of Hubbard City. Kate and her husband never missed an evening service. The pastor and Charley were invited to their home for a noon meal.

The huge living room had in it a number of small decorative tables. On every table was a Bible. The host and guests sat at the table and dined and listened to Kate's story for more than two hours. She told of her life. Charley said that there probably had never been a story comparable to that one. She said, "After we were saved, some of our former friends who lived with us in sin came to see us. I would meet them at the door and say, "I am glad to see you, but before you enter my house, I want to tell you that I have repented of my sins and God has saved me. My husband and I are trying to live for Christ. If you want to come in, we will be happy to talk to you about our experiences, but no more sinful practices or indulgences in this house." Some, she said would enter and listen, and others would turn away. Mute evidence that the same message is a savor of life unto life and of death unto death forever.

Between those great revivals in the twenties and thirties, Charley had grown much in grace, wisdom, and in understanding of methods of evangelism. A most unusual experience came to him in a revival in the Allapattah Baptist Church, Miami, Florida, in 1950. Dr. John Haldeman is the pastor. Much preparation had been made for the revival and special preparation was made for this particular occasion. The service was the unified service of the Sunday school and the 11 o'clock worship hour. Attendance goal of 1,600 in Sunday school had been set, but there were more than 2,000 registered in the classes. The pupils above the Primary Department, led by their teachers and officers, marched into the auditorium at 10:00 A.M. The building overflowed to the extent that more people were outside on the ramps than inside the auditorium. The message was of 30 minutes' duration and the invitation lasted 90 minutes, or one-and-a-half hours. There were 206 additions to the church, 168 on profession of faith. That was the largest number of additions to a church in one single service which Charley had ever witnessed. He asked one of the deacons what he thought was responsible for such an ingathering. The deflationary deacon replied, "Well, it wasn't your sermon."

He went on to say, however, that their pastor had led their church in a training program through the years and church members knew what to do. The Allapattah Baptist Church had a better training program than had been seen by Brother Matthews in any church he had visited in the Southern Baptist Convention.

The most astounding revival that Brother Charley ever witnessed or had any part in was in Havana, Cuba, in July, 1953. By then he had been serving as secretary of evangelism, either in Texas or for the Home Mission Board for seven years.

He and Mrs. Matthews had gone to Havana for the revival upon the invitation of Dr. Herbert Caudill, to help in their training school and to conduct a revival over a period of eight days. The messages were preached through an interpreter which was a new experience for Charley. The interpreter was Donald Levy, a Puerto Rican. He was the local pastor and an excellent interpreter.

A speaker's stand was erected outside the tent about 30 feet away. Loudspeaking equipment was installed so that all could hear. There were 1,200 folding chairs. Over 1,200 people were present every night and scores were responding to the invitation. On Wednesday night 142 persons made professions of faith. This was the time of the year called the rainy season in Cuba. It rained every day. If rain fell at the hour of the preaching services, the meeting was conducted in the chapel of the seminary. On Thursday night every one of the 1,200 chairs was occupied. Thick clouds hung low overhead and a torrential rain began falling. Everyone crowded under the tent, seated in the aisles and every available space from which one could escape the rain. The preachers knew that they could not be seen or heard speaking from the tent. Therefore the evangelist and his interpreter put on their raincoats and walked out on the speaker's platform in the downpour of rain. There they stood as Charley preached and Levy interpreted. The loudspeaker was alive as they began the services, so the people could hear. The water fell as an avalanche, and to give an invitation was impossible. But an invitation must be given for there were hundreds of people present who had never heard a gospel sermon before.

Charley knew that the Cubans have their own special reasons for not going out voluntarily into a rain storm. He knew that they would not come out from under that tent. But it was imperative that an invitation be given. The only hope lay in God's performing a miracle. Charley prayed this simple prayer in a moment of great faith-testing, "O God, if you love lost souls like the Bible says you do, stop this rain so an invitation can be given." In an instant rain stopped, though a dark cloud hung overhead. Ninety-two persons came out from under the tent publicly confessing their faith in Christ as Saviour. Someone made a tape recording of the service and Broadman Press made a record from the tape. It is available through Baptist Book Stores in the Southern Baptist Convention territory.

The most miraculous incident which occurred in starting a revival was in 1923 in the Baptist church at Keller, Texas. J. N. Phillips was pastor and Jerry Cox was leading the music.

The pastor had made preparation and suggested to Charley that the two of them would visit all day, having no day services. He proposed that the two of them cover a radius of four miles from the church. Then prayer would be conducted 30 minutes preceding the night service.

The meeting was cold from the first service and only four people could be reached for a prayer period in the evenings: the pastor; the bank president, a Mr. Chaney; an Intermediate boy by the name of Price who is now a pastor in Oklahoma; and Brother Matthews. The anchor dragged bottom for four or five days and the old ship of Zion could not get out to sea.

During the visiting the pastor and Charley had been twice to the home of a Baptist family, Mr. Jesse Pruett's family. Mr. and Mrs. Pruett and the older daughter had church letters in their trunks. Two visits could not move those letters. An Intermediate son in the family was lost.

On Friday the preachers had the noon meal in the home of Deacon Rhinehart. In the early afternoon Pastor Phillips suggested to Charley that he go visiting alone, and that Charley rest some and prepare his message for the night. After the pastor left, Deacon Rhinehart said something like this to Charley: "You are wasting your time here. God has forsaken Keller. You had as well pack up and go home. The town has not had a meeting in years. Last year the Methodists, the Presbyterians, and the Church of Christ all conducted revival meetings and none received a single member. The Lord has forsaken you. You had as well go."

Charley was so broken up that he felt he would die if he could not get alone with God. He picked up his Bible and went into a nearby cornfield. He opened it and read where Jesus went forth bearing his cross. (See John 19:16, 17.) Agonies over the lost and great inner fears seemed to be tearing him apart.

After reading the paragraph from his Bible he fell on his face in the dirt, crying and writhing in agony. He was there for hours. Finally peace came into his heart and he began looking for his Bible, to find that he had wallowed it into the dirt, open, where he had been reading.

Upon reaching the house, Mrs. Rhinehart anxiously inquired, "Where have you been? My husband became so uneasy he is out hunting you, for the elements are threatening."

Indeed, they were more than threatening. A small twister or cyclone swept one edge of the community. It hit only the residence of Jesse Pruett, not touching any of the other buildings on his farm. The residence was picked up, carried 65 feet, and set down on the ground. Mrs. Pruett was preparing the evening meal, and the operation was so smoothly done that not a glass of water was turned over on the table. Neither she nor her daughter was hurt.

Mr. Pruett from a distance saw what had happened and came running. As he ran into the door he shouted, "What on earth has happened?" His wife said, "A cyclone hit us, and I have already gotten the church letters out of the trunk. We are going to join the church tonight." And so they did! Their 14-year-old son followed them, having trusted Christ, and asked for baptism. Three other people were saved at the same time, making seven additions that night. That boy won a friend by the name of Satterwhite. They became students in T. C. U. Commuting, they were killed together when a train hit their car.

The next night the church would not hold the people and through Sunday the Lord poured out a great revival on Keller.

Many other great revivals cannot be mentioned, because Charley conducted revivals and simultaneous revival crusades from Cuba across the United States, including Alaska.

As long as people remember Charley Matthews, they will marvel at what God hath wrought through the phenomena of nature that three times God used the elements to further Charley's soul-winning: first, when lightning killed his Sunday school pupil; second, the cyclone at Keller, Texas; and, third, the sudden stopping of the rainstorm in Havana, Cuba.

Thus we see that God wrought through Charley Matthews in evangelism through revivals.

X

Standing for Civic Righteousness

As was indicated early in this discussion Charley had ingrained in his heart, soul, and mind a deep distaste for the dance and all unspeakable sins of sex promiscuity and murder. Therefore in Char- its accompanying evils. Those evils are multitudinous, and range from petting, undue sex familiarity, moderate drinking, on out into ley Matthews' church membership, it was easy for him to plead sobriety and abstinence from all appearance of evil.

There was first a strong stand on all moral issues within the church family. As that spirit worked its way out into the community at large, Travis Avenue Baptist Church was noted for taking its stand on all moral issues in the city and county. That stand naturally catapulted her devoted pastor into positions of leadership and great responsibility which netted for him the animosity and hatred of all those opposed to righteousness. Many incidents could not be re- corded, but among the multiple experiences encountered there was one which stands out above all others in the estimation of Dr. Mat- thews, so it is presented here. Incidentally, any local option election concerning alcoholic beverages and any other issue that could prejudice the people was sure to hear the voice of the pastor of the congregation of Travis Avenue.

Therefore, in the year 1930, when the Texas legislature legalized parimutuel gambling on horse races and dog tracks, the strong pastor of the church was pitched into the forefront of the battle.

Legalizing parimutuel gambling on horse races and dog races could not be accomplished out in the open with advance publicity. Therefore it was believed that the legislation was brought about through the influence of owners of Arlington Downs, located at Arlington, Texas, midway between Ft. Worth and Dallas. Immedi- ately following the legalizing of gambling on horse and dog races,

101

race tracks sprang up in Houston, San Antonio, and El Paso. Gambling had been outlawed so long in Texas that when the law opposing gambling was repealed (in Dr. Matthews' words, "Through diabolical trickery"), a great many people were swept off their feet by the thrill of a chance to make easy money. Public psychology or mob psychology, as it might be called, threw the people into a frenzy of anticipation. The tragedy of it all was that many church members seemed crazy to participate in betting on the races.

Politicians were supported in their political campaigns by the gambling elements and corruption took over, involving people in every walk of life. Since Arlington Downs with its big race track, one of the finest in the nation, lay between Dallas and Ft. Worth, it was inevitable that the ministerial alliance in Ft. Worth should not take this legalized vice lying down. They arose at once to fight gambling and to seek the repeal of the law that legalized it.

The fight became so extremely bitter that it raged in every session of the state legislature. The battle was carried with such intensity, and so heatedly, that more attention was given to the controversy over gambling than to all other issues that came before the lawmaking body.

Charley Matthews became the chief antagonist of gambling, and therefore the leading protagonist for repeal of legalized gambling in the area of Ft. Worth. The ministerial alliance kept him in the front line of this battle of ideas and elected him chairman of a committee to get the law repealed. Other ministers from all sections of Texas also carried the fight to Austin, the state capital. Their fight was based on the grounds that people were losing their money gambling and merchants could not collect their accounts. It was a business desecration. Not only were husbands and fathers gambling away their pay checks before reaching home, but even when the money reached the hands of the housewives, in many cases the women were gambling away the family funds and letting the grocery bills go unpaid.

Homes were being broken because the family had a wife or husband who gambled away the money that the family had looked to for sustenance. The pastor said, "A number of divorces actually took place between members of Travis Avenue Baptist Church because of these conditions. The family sustenance had been lost by the leaders in the family as they gambled away family funds at the races."

Embezzlements in banks and in other legitimate businesses by employees were occurring to an amazing degree. Suicides because of losing money and being unable to replace it, together with losses of jobs, were taking place with tragic frequency.

Here is the one story from all that happened which Dr. Matthews has agreed should go into this volume. In the membership of Travis Avenue Baptist Church was a man who was a young convert. This gentleman was a dairyman. He was head of a family of five children, ranging in age from two to ten, with a devoted wife by his side. He was invited by one of his customers to be his guest at Arlington Downs. The dairy business was at its worst in those early depression years and profits were meager. The good man, though a new convert and a member of the church, decided to take a chance. He bought a ticket for $2.00. The horse he bet on won and he made over $20.00 clear on that one parimutuel ticket which had cost him $2.00. He felt that he could try it again as it was legal. He became a frequent attendant upon the races. At first his earnings were unusually high. But the inevitable set in and he began to lose.

He finally lost all the money he collected on milk sales, all the money he had saved to pay for feed for his dairy herd. One Saturday afternoon he came home and asked his wife to go to the city with him. He excused himself down the street before going to a movie by saying he wanted to go to the drug store first. She waited for his return but instead a message came to her that her husband had drunk carbolic acid and was found dead in his car.

This tragedy struck just before the closing session of the legislature that year. Opposition to the nefarious gambling business was growing even among lawmakers. The lower house, the Representatives, had voted twice for repeal of the gambling law, but the gamblers had concentrated their influence and money on the senate which had fewer members to deal with. The bill to repeal gambling laws was before a committee in the senate.

The chairman of that committee was a lawyer from Ft. Worth who was a legal representative of Arlington Downs. Imagine a man taking a stand which would destroy his own income. One of the members of the legislature phoned Dr. Matthews and said, "That bill for the repeal of the law legalizing gambling will come up tomorrow night. You had better get your forces down here quick. We have taken a poll of the committee that has the bill. There are five against the bill and four in favor of it. If one opposed to it can be switched in favor of it, his vote will keep alive the bill. If this cannot be done, then the bill will die in the committee." Dr. Matthews tells the story:

I phoned some of the pastors and laymen asking them to appear before the committee and met with a hearty response. But that had happened so many times before and resulted in failures that I felt something unusual was necessary if we were to succeed. I lay on my bed that night praying and meditating on what to do. If ever I had a vision from God, it came to me that night. He told me to take the widow of the dairyman who had committed suicide and her five children to Austin, to secret them in a hotel room until the hour that the senate committee would convene, then to get in touch with Senator G. H. Nelson from Lubbock, Texas. Senator Nelson was a Baptist layman. The Lord instructed me to get him to present the little family that gambling had robbed of its father and husband, and one of the committee members who was opposed to the bill would change his vote.

The next morning I went to the dairy farm and presented my proposition to the family. They agreed to go with me to Austin, and to do anything they could to help. The trip was made. Senator Nelson was contacted and he agreed to present the lady and her children to the committee in his speech which was to be the last thing before a vote was taken. I shall never forget that hour that night. Such drama had seldom ever been seen in a lawmaking chamber. The senate chamber was full to overflowing. People were there from all over Texas: gamblers, politicians, lawmakers, ranchmen, bankers, church people, people of all walks of life. Attention gripped every heart. The committee assembled. The governor, James B. Allred, was sitting near the committee. Two former governors were sitting near him. Governor Allred, a Christian, was using his influence to the fullest extent that the bill would be kept alive.

The debate burst forth in all its fury. I was slated to speak, but because of having appeared so many times before the legislature on other occasions, I asked a pastor from San Antonio, Texas, to take my place. He had only five minutes for his talk and he was not accustomed to making speeches on such an occasion. He said,

"An old lady in my church told me of a man that had committed suicide because he lost all his savings while gambling on horse races." That was about all he said. He was followed by the last speaker, who was to speak against the bill—and for gambling.

That speaker who opposed the repeal bill was himself a race horse owner and a noted lawyer. He said, "The only grounds that our opponents have stated for repealing the law that has legalized gambling on horse races, was that some old woman had told someone that somebody had committed suicide because he lost money on a horse race. Gentlemen of this committee, I will make you this proposition, if anyone is here that could prove that anyone ever committed suicide because he lost money on a horse race, we will concede victory to the opposition."

Why he ever made such a statement can be accredited to only one thing, God was in charge.

The speaker sat down. It was then time for Senator Nelson to make the last appeal for the passing of the bill to repeal legalized gambling. Such a dramatic hour shall probably not be seen in a legislative hall for a long while, if ever. Senator Nelson, the last speaker, was ready. He opened his address with these words, "Honorable members of the committee, Governor Allred, members of our lawmaking body, and citizens of Texas; the opponents of this bill that would repeal legalized gambling in the state of Texas have just issued a challenge to you who render this most important decision that affects business, morals, and the entire social order of our great republic. Remember he is asking you who will decide whether this bill is to be kept alive or whether it will be killed to base your conclusion on just one proposition, namely, that it be proved that anyone ever committed suicide because he lost his money betting on a horse race."

The senator turned and called in a voice which could be heard across the senate chamber and said, "Mrs. Orr, come here please and bring your children with you." The widow and her children were seated in a distant part of the senate floor, 100 feet from where the committee members sat. The sight of that lovely mother and her five little fatherless children following her across that Senate floor was the most powerful demonstration I have ever witnessed. She was leading the baby boy by the hand. Senator Nelson held that little curly-headed boy in his arms. He faced the committee and made the most dramatic appeal, I think, that I have ever heard. He said, "I hate to do this for the family's sake. But gentlemen of this committee, do you believe that this little boy deserves a daddy? His daddy is not here today. He is dead. He lost his money, all that he had to support this family that he loved more than he loved his life. He could not face the tragedy of this disaster of losing his money in betting on horse races, and because of that he took his own life. Am I right lady?" Mrs. Orr said, "Yes."

At that moment a member of the committee, the senator from Rockwall, near Dallas, Texas, buried his face in his hands. He was a Christian, but he had voted against the bill. When Senator Nelson concluded his brief speech, the chairman of the committee called for a vote. The senator from Rockwall voted aye and the bill was kept alive by a vote of five to four, exactly as God had revealed to Charley. God had vindicated the thought in the mind of Charley Matthews that God was speaking to him the night before as he wrestled with God while on his bed back home. But the fight was not over. The gambling forces die hard. The committee chairman did not present the bill to the body for a vote. The session closed and the lawmakers went home.

But Governor Allred called a special session of the legislature with only one bill to consider. That bill was the one to repeal legalized gambling on horse races and dog races. The bill passed both houses and legalized gambling was killed in Texas we believe forever.

The special session of the legislature cost the taxpayers of Texas $10,000.00 but it was worth ten times that much. All the race tracks went out of business. Recently, in 1955, Arlington Downs was sold to a business syndicate for six million dollars and on it will be constructed legitimate business enterprises with a great section being opened for the construction of residences. Thus what was once a curse will turn out to be a help to provide honest toil for a host of families in this great section of Texas.

Yes, God wrought in mysterious way his wonders to perform in civic righteousness through the leadership and companionship of Charley Matthews.

All the Orr children and the aged grandfather were later saved and baptized into the fellowship of the Travis Avenue Baptist Church. Thus God wrought in blessing the man who waited to see that he is God (Ps. 46:10), and who relied upon God for wisdom.

XI

A Program of Evangelism

The life story of a man whose origin was in poverty, obscurity, and ill health, but who has been used mightily of God in the gospel ministry for 35 years, the last ten of which ushered in a new day in evangelism for Southern Baptists, must be witnessed to by more than one man. The continent has felt the impact from Panama to Alaska.

Can another instance be found where a man who had no high school diploma; never matriculated in a college of arts and sciences nor a university; and dropped out of the seminary at the halfway mark, was given an LL.D. degree by a university 102 years old? "It happened in Texas!"

Charley was secretary of evangelism for the Texas Baptist General Convention. He was in a revival meeting with R. C. Campbell and the First Baptist Church, Columbia, South Carolina. The telephone rang in his hotel room.

When he answered, the university president took for granted that Charley would recognize his familiar voice, so did not introduce himself. But what he said stunned Charley so that he thought one of his "preacher boys," W. Fred Swank, Fort Worth, was kidding him! Too, his modesty would not let him believe what he was hearing: "Could you preach the commencement sermon for Baylor? We want to confer upon you a doctor's degree."

Believing Swank was talking, Charley jovially answered back with what he regarded as equal nonsense. Then the president kidded, "What size hat do you wear? I doubt if it will be big enough!"

Then President Pat M. Neff of Baylor University (founded in 1845) soberly asked, "Charley which degree would you prefer, D. D. or LL. D.?" When Charley could speak again he meekly said, 'Why, the LL.D. I suppose." During the writing of this volume he confessed to the writer that he had wished often that he had taken the D. D.

In the mid-thirties, in the very depth of the great depression, Southern Baptists were suffering severe depression at two points. First, in their finances, Southern Baptist churches were suffering. Second, in baptisms Southern Baptists stood at an unprecedented low. World War II followed and baptisms became fewer still. All over the Southern Baptist Convention territory, earnest men of God were crying out for guidance and for help. Following that hour of travail, God gave Southern Baptists what is without doubt and without any semblance of exaggeration, the greatest program of evangelism known to the Christian faith. This program was born of the Spirit of God. It had its roots in the hearts of many personalities, some of whom were: J. B. Lawrence, executive secretary and treasurer of the Home Mission Board; M. E. Dodd, past president of the Southern Baptist Convention, pastor of the First Baptist Church of Shreveport, Louisiana; L. R. Scarborough, president of the Southwestern Seminary; R. C. Campbell, executive secretary of the Texas Baptist General Convention; and Charles Everett Matthews, pastor of Travis Avenue Baptist Church, Ft. Worth, Texas.

A word of explanation and of defense of both the program and Brother Matthews himself is in order at this point. Following the writing of the first edition of the book, *The Southern Baptist Program of Evangelism* by C. E. Matthews, the writer of this volume heard criticism from Florida to California after this manner: "Oh, well, that is Charley Matthews' program," or "Brother Matthews gave us this program which we ought to follow," etc., etc.

In defense of the program, let us say, first, that it is not the conception of any one man. It is not a man-originated program. In the second place, let us say that Charley Matthews was only one in a group thinking and praying, and to whom God said the same thing. The program was given of God's Holy Spirit. God wrought upon the hearts of many.

As Southern Baptists cried to God, there is no hesitancy in saying that the same voice of God spoke to C. E. Matthews on September 28, 1936, and delivered to him by direct revelation the heart of the Southern Baptist Program of Evangelism. When the Holy Spirit spoke to Simon Peter, he opened the gospel door for the Gentile world and it began forever the movement that has resulted in the salvation of men, women, and children without number from that time and will until the end of the world. So has this program of evangelism reached increasing multitudes, and should so continue.

The Lord did not reveal to Andrew, John, James, or Thomas his will concerning the evangelism of the Gentiles. He loved them just as he loved Peter, but they evidently did not have the dogged determination to carry out the program of God concerning the evangelization of the heathen world as Peter did. We do not believe that Peter was more righteous than the other apostles, or that he was the appointed head over the others and over the church. In fact, he was so impulsive and at times so weak that when the angel said to the women at the open sepulcher, "Go tell the disciples" about the resurrection, he added, "and Peter." Evidently Peter's way of living had caused others to doubt his discipleship. After his swearing and his denial of Jesus, he needed a special word in order to hold him from the suicide's grave into which Judas Iscariot had plunged when he realized that he had sold "the innocent blood."

All this is said to give emphasis to the fact that C. E. Matthews laid no claim to perfection. Evidently the revelation to him, concerning the program of evangelism, which he believed has already been proved as coming directly from God, did not come to him because of his being more righteous than other men; but God knew the particular elements essential in a person in the carrying through of the program in spite of the hindrances and the obstacles which are sure to be met on every hand. And let no one think that Charley Matthews did not meet hindrances and obstacles!

On one occasion while he was bringing a series of messages in a cultural center where a great Baptist University had been established decades before, Charles observed that each time he stood up to speak, a certain group of men walked out through the door. His quick eye revealed to him that the same men left each time. He asked the master of ceremonies who they were and why they were leaving. The answer was, "They are the intelligentsia, and they think they can get nothing from a man who does not use words that are difficult to understand."

That is comparable to what a freshman student in Southwestern

Baptist Seminary said the opening night of the only full session Charley attended. Dr. George W. Truett had finished the address of the evening. He was in his ripe, rich prime, at his full best, and his message had stunned, awed, inspired, broken the hearts and encouraged many of us. Intermittently people wept, rejoiced, yearned to be like Jesus, and prayed for strength to do his work. So silent were the exits and the hallways that the staccato voice of the critic could be heard: "So that's George Truett, is it? Huh, I'd heard of him clear over into my state. I came to Texas hoping I'd hear him. WHY, HE DIDN'T USE ONE WORD I COULDN'T UNDERSTAND!"

Charley knew open opposition, and sinister sly attacks of snipers who have sought to bring down the program of evangelism or to bring him down. Only the same dogged persistence which made it impossible for the family to pull him from under the cover at the foot of the bed at age three, and the determination which put him through business college, rebuilt his body into that of an athlete, and marked his surrender to preach at the age of 34—only these qualities enabled him to carry on for the glory of God, increasing Southern Baptists in number and unifying Southern Baptists around their main business, evangelism.

Now let Charley tell in his own words how God spoke to him:

One day in 1936, the Jewish evangelist, Hyman Appleman, was in conference with me and the subject we were discussing was evangelism. I stated in the beginning that it appeared to me that the simultaneous crusades on the associational level came nearer meeting every phase of the New Testament evangelism than any other method. Brother Appleman agreed with me, but said, "There is too much jealousy among pastors and churches for the simultaneous method to succeed." All these things were food for thought.

The literal truth of Appleman's words has been observed. A few days after this conversation, exactly on the morning of September 28, 1936, I was in my study preparing a funeral message for a sainted mother, Mrs. E. J. Tarlton. All of a sudden I found my mind centered on evangelism and completely lost my thoughts in meditation on the subject. Suddenly there came to me a complete program of evangelism as though I had read it all in a flash from a book. It was so vividly indelibled in my mind that not a semblance of it has ever left me. I was so electrified by the experience that I wanted to tell everyone that I met. Dr. Frank Murrell, pastor at Denison,

110

Texas, First Baptist Church, was to assist in Mrs. Tarleton's funeral. I met him upon his arrival and told him my experience. He was as enthusiastic about it as I was. He said, "Brother Matthews, tell Dr. Campbell about it and let's carry that program out in Texas." That evening Mrs. Matthews and I went into Dallas to see Dr. R. C. Campbell who was then executive secretary of the Baptist General Convention of Texas.

"We found Dr. Campbell sitting in the auditorium of the First Baptist Church waiting for an evangelistic service to begin in which Gypsy Smith, Sr., was to preach. There were several minutes before time for the service to begin, and I immediately told Dr. Campbell of my experience with the Lord. The inspiration of it must have been conclusive, for Dr. Campbell became so thrilled that he said, "Charley, we will put that program on in Texas next year."

Then he said, "Meet me and Dr. Scarborough at Dr. Scarborough's house at 3:00 P.M. tomorrow." The three of us met at the appointed time. But the Lord who spoke to both Cornelius and Simon Peter was speaking to Dr. Campbell, too. He said, "Let's have an evangelistic conference for our preachers here and get this program started." Then he said, "I am appointing the three of us as a committee on evangelism, with Brother Matthews as chairman. The first thing we must do is to write a program for the evangelistic conference." The conference idea belonged entirely to Dr. Campbell. God had spoken to him the night before, giving him the conference idea. I wrote down the conference program line by line.

The program was dictated to me immediately by Dr. Scarborough as if the voice of God uttered it. He recited it as though he were reading it from a paper, giving the theme, the topics for discussion, and all. I never heard anything like it in logic and in continuity of thought. The conference was held in the seminary chapel in June, 1937. It was attended by about 700 men.

That was the first statewide evangelistic conference ever conducted by any group of Southern Baptists. Not only has it been repeated every year since that time in Texas, but for years similar conferences have been conducted as statewide affairs in every state convention in the Southern Baptist Convention.

The program of evangelism as revealed to Dr. Matthews on September 28, 1936, was as follows:

I. Organizational

   1. An employed secretary of evangelism in the state
      to supervise the program. (Remember this was a
      Texas program.)

2. An associational chairman in every association to supervise the work of evangelism on an associational level.
3. An evangelism church council in every church to plan and direct evangelism on a church level.

II. Promotional
1. A statewide evangelistic conference each year.
2. An annual simultaneous revival crusade in every association.

The simultaneous revival program from beginning to end as he understood it is found in the book, *The Southern Baptist Program of Evangelism.*

The vision as received by Dr. Matthews in his study on September 28, 1936, became a reality. The year 1937 was a banner year in baptisms, resulting in glorious revivals in churches from the largest cities to the most remote rural part-time churches of Texas.

The Holy Spirit moved in other hearts. As stated before, the Spirit of God was rooting the program of evangelism in the hearts of Baptists throughout the Southern Baptist Convention. The strange thing about it was that just as the sections of the Bible written by men fit together in one great program detailing the birth, death, ascension, and the second advent of Jesus, so the Spirit of God working in the hearts of multitudes of Baptists finally consummated and crystallized revelation into one identical program. That program is revolutionizing the work of evangelizing and is here to stay.

Some of the experiences must be mentioned to show how the Spirit of God operated in bringing about this program; to show that the program is not a man-made idea, and that Charley Matthews was not the only one who heard the voice of God, so it cannot be called his program of evangelism. God spoke to him, and God spoke to others.

Prior to the meeting of the Southern Baptist Convention in Richmond, Virginia, in 1938, Brother Matthews was in a revival in Portales, New Mexico. He had written a resolution to be offered at the Convention concerning a Convention-wide crusade in 1939. The success of the 1937 crusade in Texas had inspired the heart of this great pastor-evangelist to share what God had wrought with the other states of the Southern Convention territory. He had completed plans to attend the Convention, but was stricken with a severe attack of sinus following a blinding dust storm at Portales. Being in excruciating pain, he decided that his physical condition would make it impossible for him to attend this Convention. He reconsidered and went. He showed his resolution to President J. R. Sampey. He declined consideration. He then took it to Pat M. Neff, president of Baylor University, Waco, Texas, and chairman of the resolutions committee. In counsel with L. R. Scarborough and the resolutions committee, slight changes were made.

The recommendation was read to the Convention by Pat M. Neff of Texas. Convention President Sampey introduced Dr. Neff by saying, "Dr. Neff has a resolution submitted by a most enthusiastic pastor brother." Neff read it, and it was adopted, as follows: (Abridged)

FIRST—That we, the messengers of the Southern Baptist Convention, definitely commit ourselves to put on, by the help of God, an extensive and intensive campaign of soul-winning during 1939 with intensive and organized effort to reach all areas of the South, all of our churches, mission stations, and communities.

SECOND—That an organization be set up in the Southern Baptist Convention to enlist all the state, associational, and church organizations, challenging the best there is in all of us to that end. And, that Dr. Roland Q. Leavell, Superintendent of Evangelism of the Home Mission Board, and the President-elect of the Convention, shall lead in the movement. And that we urge every agency of the Southern Baptist Convention to share in its promotion. (SBC *Annual,* 1938, p. 64.)

IT CALLED FOR A CONVENTION-WIDE CRUSADE. Dr. Ed Solomon moved that the crusade be jointly led by the newly-elected president of the Convention and Roland Q. Leavell, superintendent of evangelism of the Home Mission Board, of the Southern Baptist Convention, in 1938.

The adoption of that resolution resulted in two distinct things: first, a new record in baptisms that year (1939): 263,155; second it created for the first time the idea of a unified effort in evangelism for churches of the Southern Baptist Convention.

War broke out in Europe in 1939, and for the following years the world was in the grip of bloody World War II. The United States was in the war from 1941 to 1945. Therefore, the next step toward completing the Southern Baptist Program of Evangelism did not come until the Convention met in Atlanta, Georgia, in 1944.

A committee of 18 men from 18 states reported on evangelism. W. H. Knight, chairman, read the report. Alarming conditions stood out (total report, Southern Baptist Convention *Annual,* 1944, pages 78-80). That committee did not have the 1943 totals. But in 1943 the figures hit an all-time low of one baptism to 27.6 members. Something had to be done—God was speaking.

The committee's third recommendation was:

3. That this Convention appoint a special committee on Evangelism representing all the cooperating states, to work with the Evangelistic Department of the Home Mission Board and leaders of our Sunday School Board in planning a great Southwide Evangelistic campaign for our Centennial year of 1945. Machinery should be organized, covering the entire Convention, that would sponsor the ideal of at least one revival in every church throughout the South in 1945. This committee would be instructed to call upon all agencies of the Convention and all State Boards to join in the promotion of this campign. No greater Memorial of a century of Baptist history could be erected than that we should strive toward a goal of one million baptisms during our centennial year.

A special committee on evangelism was named. The First Baptist Church of Shreveport was asked to lend its pastor, M. E. Dodd, to the Convention to spearhead the Centennial year goal of 1,000,000 baptisms in 1945.

Dr. Dodd spent about seven months of that year in the field, promoting as one man this great crusade to baptize 1,000,000 converts in 12 months. The effort was far from successful and the reports revealed only 256,699 baptisms in 1945.

The results broke the heart of Dr. Dodd, but the Holy Spirit was leading in his own way toward God's program, and the failure turned out to be a glorious contribution toward the goal. By midsummer of 1945, Dr. Dodd was smarting under the apparent defeat. He was overburdened with a sense of failure and was suffering a broken heart in his great compassionate soul as he remembered the lost who were not being reached. It was then, the summer of

1945 while C. E. Matthews was pastor of Travis Avenue, that he received a call from Dr. Dodd. Dodd said, "Charley, can you catch that early morning plane out of Dallas and come to my office in the morning? I want to have a full day's conference with you and W. H. Knight." Knight was executive secretary of the Louisiana Baptist Convention.

Dr. Matthews made the trip. The conference opened at 8:00 A.M. in Dr. Dodd's study. Lunch was served from the pastor's desk, and the conference lasted throughout the day. Brethren Knight, Dodd, and Matthews had as their secretary, Mrs. Ira Prosser (secretary to Dr. Dodd) who remained throughout the day and took every word in shorthand. At the end of the day, Dr. Dodd was ready to speak. His laconic remarks were the words of a broken-hearted man.

Dr. Dodd said, "Brethren, I have worked my heart out in this crusade, but we are getting nowhere. I have just returned from a crusade in Baltimore, Maryland. Maryland used to be a Baptist stronghold. We have lost Maryland. We scarcely had enough results in the crusade to count. You men have directed simultaneous crusades and I am convinced that the simultaneous methods fit completely with the New Testament efforts in all that the churches of that day actually did. Their work was unified, they worked together, and their effort was church centered."

Overwhelmed by the great lethargy in evangelism which he had observed in Maryland and across the Convention territory, Dr. Dodd turned to Brother Matthews and spoke as follows:

"Charley, you have had good results in Texas in crusades. What Southern Baptists need is a PROGRAM. We do not have a program of evangelism. I want you to tell me about what you have in your mind about a program." Brother Matthews went over his experience in the revelation he had received on September 28, 1936. He discussed the evangelistic conferences and the crusades which followed. Dr. Knight said, "That is what I believe. That program will work."

Brother Matthews summed up the day's labor by saying, "With a few minor alterations, that is fundamentally the program we have today."

Dr. Dodd became jubilant in spirit as he envisioned the future for Southern Baptists with a program of evangelism and said, almost in an ecstasy, "Brethren, I wish Southern Baptists would elect me secretary of evangelism. I would like to give this program a try." That was not God's will. Dr. Dodd was ill then and not physically able to promote the program. For further details, see *The Southern Baptist Program of Evangelism*, 1956 edition, Convention Press, p. VI.

Even while Dr. J. B. Lawrence, executive secretary-treasurer of the Home Mission Board, was struggling through the years to pay the staggering debt upon the Board and re-establish its credit on the one hand and operate an aggressive home mission program on the other hand, God was revealing to him his program of evangelism. Let him tell you in his own words in a letter to the writer, July 31, 1956:

You want to know how I arrived at the conviction that Southern Baptists must adopt a program of evangelism with state departments giving permanency thereto. That idea was a development in my thinking as I considered the task of evangelism under the Home Mission Board; in fact, it came to me when I was thinking about re-establishing the Home Mission Board Department of Evangelism under Dr. Leavell. I knew that we could not have a corps of evangelists and, in my thinking, it dawned on me as a sort of revelation that we did not need a corp of evangelists and singers; what we needed was a program and a man to put on the program. This program was not fully developed in my mind when we elected Dr. Leavell. That part of the program, however, which pertained to the corps of evangelists was fully developed. At that time I talked to Dr. Pope, the executive secretary of Tennessee, about the method that I had in mind for the Evangelistic Department, which method was to have only a directive force and to work in cooperation with the state mission boards. He was favorable to this idea.

Dr. Lawrence recounts how God wrought to select Matthews:

When the Home Mission Board had paid its debt, and was ready to establish the Evangelistic Department permanently (and the Southern Baptist Convention had adopted a Program of Evangelism and asked the Home Mission Board to finance it), I began thinking seriously of the man whom we would employ as the director. There were a number of men that could do the work. But I did not want any one of them unless he felt a divine call from the Lord to take the place offered. Therefore, before I wrote any of these men I prayed to the Lord that he would not let any of them even consider

116

the position if he was not called of the Lord. We wanted God's man in this particular field. I contacted three men, but as I signed the letter to each one I prayed that the Lord would not let him accept if he was not the man for the place. Each one of these three in succession wrote back immediately that he was committed to the pastorate and felt that it would not be advisable for him to consider the position.

Someone suggested, I do not now know who that someone was, that the man for the place was C. E. Matthews, the superintendent of evangelism in Texas. I made some inquiry and found from all sources that he surely was the man. I wrote him a letter and asked him if he was interested to come to Atlanta so that we could have a conference. I got his letter saying that he would come to consult with me about the position. I shall never forget the first sentence that he spoke after greeting me. That sentence was, "I was looking for your letter."

We discussed the position. I said nothing to him about my desire to have a Baptist type of evangelism, except that I was of the opinion that what Southern Baptists needed was a specific Baptist type of evangelism in doctrine and practice. He agreed with me that what we needed was a Baptist type of evangelism.

I never suggested to him at any time what he should do in the field of evangelism. I only prayed for him. He proceeded under the leading of the Spirit to develop a distinctive Baptist type of evangelism and to put it into practice. I watched him as he proceeded and noted with joy and approval his progress. What he did in the field of evangelism has revolutionized the denominational thought and activity of Southern Baptists and given an impetus to evangelism that has startled the denominations of the United States. Many of them are adopting the program he developed for themselves.

I have worked with him in the closest spirit of harmony and cooperation. He has been, so far as I have been able to see, an ideal in the field of denominational evangelism. He has done a wonderful work for Baptists.

That God wrought in establishing the Southern Baptist Program of Evangelism is conclusive in that simultaneous revivals have been conducted in every state in the Southern Baptist Convention, in all associations, and outside the local boundaries in Alaska, Rio de Janiero, Old Mexico, Argentina, Paraguay, Uruguay, and Nigeria, as well as Panama and Cuba. All states use secretaries of evangelism; the associations elect an evangelism chairman annually; and the churches increasingly follow the program as a working model.

XII

For Southern Baptists

It is now fitting that we present a bit of history of what God hath wrought among Southern Baptists since they adopted a program of evangelism in 1947. Here is a brief summary:

In no like period of Southern Baptist history have such records been made in winning people to Christ through his servants as during the first nine years of the Southern Baptist Program of Evangelism. Not one of those who have participated in the promotion of this program would claim personal credit for these marvelous results. Unitedly, without exception, we believe that everyone would say in rejoicing sincerity, "To God be the glory."

We are persuaded that Baptists as a whole do not realize what these astounding accomplishments are. God's blessings upon Southern Baptists during these nine years of the operation of the Program of Evangelism compel the belief that God will continue to bless Southern Baptists, pastors and churches together, as they unitedly press forward as a mighty army for God under the leadership of the present secretary of the Department of Evangelism, Dr. Leonard Sanderson, who succeeded Dr. Matthews, January 1, 1956. For the sake of enlightenment, edification, and inspiration for the people called Southern Baptists, we give as follows a brief summary of what God hath wrought through the Southern Baptist Program of Evangelism, from its adoption in 1947 through 1955, inclusive:

First, through the use of church organizations:

1. Through the Sunday Schools

The greatest soul-winning organizations in the history of the Christian religion in churches are the Sunday schools in our Southern Baptist churches. The work of the Sunday schools has been capably led by the indomitable J. N. Barnett, secretary of the Sunday School Department of the Sunday School Board. His books,

One to Eight and *The Pull of the People*, plus his leadership to "enroll a million more in '54" have greatly reinforced evangelism. There has been close co-operation of all.

The Southern Baptist Program of Evangelism supplements the Sunday school in a definite way. The program calls for the taking of a religious census on an association-wide basis, thereby enlarging the enrollment, bringing the lost under the influence of Bible teaching, and then conducting High Attendance Day in the Sunday school during the revival meeting. On these high attendance days following the taking of the census, thousands of our churches year after year break all previous Sunday school attendance records. On that day also, a unified service is conducted through the Sunday school period linked with the morning preaching service in which hundreds of thousands of boys and girls and men and women have accepted Christ as Saviour, rededicated their lives, and united with the churches for baptism and by letter.

2. Through the Training Unions

Through the influence of the Training Union, led by Jerry Lambdin, secretary of that department for the Sunday School Board, the Training Unions in Southern Baptist churches have experienced unprecedented growth numerically and in the training of our people. The Training Union Department during this period has adopted a training course in the study of soul-winning. Two of the books used in this course were written by C. E. Matthews: namely, *Every Christian's Job* and *A Church Revival*. There have been 215,952 copies of the first book sold, and 131,986 copies of the second.

A better-trained membership is better able to do personal work and visitation preceding revivals and during revivals. Therefore the Training Unions have been more dynamic in their active ministries of reaching the lost and unaffiliated for Christ.

In addition, the Southern Baptist Program of Evangelism has augmented these achievements by using the Training Unions in the thousands of revivals conducted under its auspices by aiding Training Unions in the churches to break attendance records, and by special nights for Training Unions during revivals.

Greatest of all, probably, is the inspiration which came to the Training Union Department through the Southern Baptist Program of Evangelism which resulted in the writing of the book, *Your Life and Your Church,* used so effectively in the conservation of evangelism.

3. Through the Department of Church Music

Singing praises to God and singing the experiences of the redeemed have always been a part of the Christian religion. The program of evangelism of the Southern Baptist Convention took note of this fact and set out to capture evangelistic music for the program. E. Powell Lee was brought into the Department of Evangelism to promote music. His inspiring leadership has joined the capable talent of the music department of the Sunday School Board. Dr. Hines Sims and his staff have co-operated eagerly and most helpfully in the promotion of the right kind of music for revivals and soul-winning. They have appeared on statewide evangelistic conference programs and discussed the relationship between music and evangelism.

At the request of the state secretaries of evangelism the music department of the Sunday School Board produced a song book titled *Crusade Songs* for use in revivals. This book of 150 pages has been used extensively throughout our Convention. In church and mission revivals 94,684 copies have been sold. The department also publishes *The Church Musician,* a monthly music magazine for use in the churches of the Convention.

Two thirds of the states of our Convention are now organized with a music department, paralleling the other departments and are vigorously promoting an adequate church music program. The state secretary of music and the associational directors are seeking to reach every church with a well-rounded program of gospel music for revivals and soul-winning. Increasing emphasis is placed upon congregational singing, and evangelism through singing.

4. Through the Woman's Missionary Union

This dynamic evangelistic unit in our churches is turning more and more to personal witnessing and evangelism in the communities where the churches are located. Women realize more keenly day by day, that being missionary overseas means being missionary over the streets, or over the hilltops on the other side of the community. Therefore, Woman's Missionary Union is redoubling its community missions efforts in full co-operation and stubborn determination to become a dynamic factor in soul-winning in every church.

In the official statement of "Aims for Advancement," Christian witnessing plays a prominent part. Community missions receives great emphasis in the WMU Plan of Work, as stated in the *1956-1957 Year Book*. The Number One purpose of community missions according to the statement is "to win souls." Soul-winning is promoted by:

(1) Co-operation with the church in carrying out Southern Baptist plans for evangelism
(2) Individual efforts in personal soul-winning
(3) Prayer meetings in homes
(4) Planned soul-winning visitation
(5) Mission Sunday school classes
(6) Vacation Bible schools for unchurched groups
(7) Work in Good Will Centers
(8) Services in hospitals, jails, and other institutions
(9) Distribution of Bibles and other religious literature

The community missions committee in each church composed of a chairman and the community missions chairman from each circle, in addition to other duties, is to "Lead members in making a survey of the community with special reference to the unsaved and unchurched people . . ." and to "seek to enlist every member in some definite activity for soul-winning."

In preparation for revivals the WMU, in addition to sponsoring cottage prayer meetings, has often taken the names of all women and girl prospects and had them visited through the community missions organization.

Miss Alma Hunt, executive secretary, Mrs. R. L. Mathis, president, and Mrs. William McMurray, secretary of the Department of Missionary Fundamentals, have expressed themselves very forcibly concerning their interest in the work of evangelism.

5. Through the Brotherhood

One of the four foundation stones upon which Brotherhood builds is a cornerstone of evangelism. The Brotherhood has worked at this in a profitable way by conducting hundreds of thousands of cottage prayer meetings in preparation for revivals. Men have observed special nights in revivals for the Brotherhood. They have participated in revival visitation and in perennial visitation around the calendar in their church fields. They have inspired one of the most dynamic contributions of Brotherhood to simultaneous revivals, in the conducting of a great associational rally for men immediately preceding the date of a crusade.

In the second place, the Southern Baptist Program of Evangelism has influenced churches in general.

1. The Southern Baptist Program of Evangelism has provided and offered instructions for all our churches, from the downtown city church to the church in the most remote section in America in the following helpful ways:

(1) How to prepare a church for a revival
(2) How to carry on the performance of a revival
(3) How to attract the lost and the unaffiliated members to the revival services through publicity, visitation, pack-a-pew, prospect dinner, special nights for each organization, and all the methods known in evangelism.
(4) Teaching evangelism to church members
(5) Conserving the results of evangelism
(6) Best of all, a practical, effective program of perennial evangelism throughout the year, led through the Church Council of Evangelism.

So effective has been the work of the Southern Baptist Program of Evangelism that churches reporting no baptisms, numbering 5,996 in 1946, with a ratio of one baptism to 24 members, have changed to 4,799 churches baptizing no one in 1955, and a ratio of one baptism to 20.3 members. And this in the face of the fact that there were 3,976 more Baptist churches in 1955 than in 1946!

2. The Southern Baptist Program of Evangelism has wrought for the pastors of the Convention.

We believe that the greatest blessings of God in the Southern Baptist Program of Evangelism have been given to the pastors of the churches. They have been instructed, inspired, and developed into flaming evangelists for Christ in the following ways:

(1) By learning effective methods in evangelism
(2) By learning how to build and deliver evangelistic sermons

(3) Through conserving the results of evangelism by conducting personally a class for new members, teaching *Your Life and Your Church*

(4) By developing confidence and convictions to the extent that they conduct revivals in their own churches throughout our Convention. It has been said, "Help a pastor and you touch an entire church membership."

This remarkable and amazing feat has been accomplished through:

(1) Permanent organization; state secretaries and associational chairmen of evangelism

(2) Conducting fellowship clinics during simultaneous crusades

(3) Conducting annual associational clinics

(4) Using the Church Council of Evangelism

(5) The annual statewide evangelistic conference

In the statewide evangelistic conferences, pastors and others have been privileged to learn up-to-date methods in evangelism, and to sit at the feet and listen to such spiritual giants as Robert G. Lee, W. A. Criswell, J. D. Grey, Ramsey Pollard, Perry F. Webb, Robert E. Naylor, H. H. Hobbs, Carl Bates, and scores of others who have given their very life's blood to the cause of evangelism and to the sharing with the brethren of their all in the interest of winning lost souls to our Saviour.

Take a brief look at what God hath wrought through the Southern Baptist Program of Evangelism throughout the denomination as a whole.

1. Baptisms

In the nine years preceding the adoption of the Southern Baptist Program of Evangelism, 1938-1946, total baptisms were 2,120,773. The first nine years of the Program of Evangelism, 1947-1955, baptisms totaled 3,211,823, a total gain of 1,091,050 baptisms in the second nine-year period. That is an average gain of 121,228 baptisms per year for the nine years of the Program of Evangelism. (See SBC *Handbook*, 1956, p. 57.)

2. Revivals

The great emphasis upon more revivals led to an average of

one and a half revivals per church during the year of 1955, or a total of 45,658 revivals conducted in our 30,377 churches. Two Convention-wide simultaneous revival crusades have been conducted; the first in 1950-1951, and the second in 1955. In 1955, more than 22,000 churches engaged in revivals over a period of six weeks. Total baptisms were above 200,000 and more than 100,000 united with churches by transfer of membership. This undoubtedly was the greatest crusade from the standpoint of visible results in the history of the Christian religion. Total baptisms in 1955 were 416,867.

3. Every Phase of Denominational Activity

In the atmosphere of revival, stewardship and promotion are at new highs. During these crusades and in individual church revivals thousands of young people have surrendered for special service: foreign missions, home missions, pastors, educational directors, ministers of music, and other phases of dedicated living for Jesus Christ in the homeland and overseas.

4. In Solidifying and Unifying Southern Baptists

Before the adoption of the Program of Evangelism, there were often heard discussions of the possibility of a division of the Southern Baptist Convention. That division might follow geographical lines, with the Mississippi River as the central boundary. Others thought that Southern Baptists might break up into groups differing over theology. Since the great simultaneous crusade in 1950, the writer has heard no further remarks, and certainly nothing is seen in print. It is believed that Southern Baptists are a unit in evangelism at home and overseas as never before.

5. Book Stores

God hath wrought a special blessing upon our Baptist book stores through the Southern Baptist Program of Evangelism. During these nine years the total sales of revival promotion materials—streamers, bumper cards, bulletin board posters, billboards, postal cards, lapel buttons, and every special medium of publicity—have greatly increased the volume of the book stores. Increased sales of study course books, books of evangelistic sermons, song books, and books affecting every phase of church life stimulated by evangelism could be summed up in millions of dollars.

The amazing story of sales of materials directly connected with the work of evangelism can be seen in a glance at the following report furnished by Odell Crowe of the Merchandise Selection Department of the Sunday School Board:

Form E-1 Prospect Card, 1,976,585; Form E-4 "Christ is the Answer" gummed sticker, 1,074,150; Form E-51 Revival Poster, 410,396; Day-Glo Car Bumper Strips 4 inches x 15 inches, 306,216; Taxi Cards, 6,139; Window Cards, 131,490; Revival Post Cards, 772,876; Pastor's Letter, 140,641; Billboard Poster, 4,107; Lapel Buttons—"Christ is the Answer," 80,316; Day-Glo Directional Arrows, 147,681; Prospect Card E-7, 344,239; E-6 Personal Worker's Assignment Card, 254,313; Attendance Chain E-3, 999,149; E-2 Training Union Attendance Chain, 415,202; Cloth Street Banner, 1-178; All-Purpose Poster, 5,322; Evangelistic Blotters, 397,445.

Books: *Every Christian's Job,* 215,952; *A Church Revival,* 131,-986; *Southern Baptist Program of Evangelism* (52 issue), 14,455; *Southern Baptist Program of Evangelism* (56 issue), 3,300; *Your Life and Your Church,* 441,401.

There were 8,274,539 pieces of merchandise promoting our Program of Evangelism sold by our book stores during the leadership of Dr. Matthews.

6. Special Contributions

Many of our people, influenced by the Program of Evangelism, make large contributions to the promotion of evangelism. Chief of these are Mr. and Mrs. William Fleming of Fort Worth, Texas, whose generous contributions during this period in a material way to the cause of evangelism could be regarded as the largest of any ever made by any couple to the cause of evangelism in the history of the Southern Baptist Convention.

7. Scholastically

The influence of the Southern Baptist Program of Evangelism is now reaching into the classrooms of our colleges and seminaries, where the book, *The Southern Baptist Program of Evangelism,* is being taught in class or is used as required reading during the courses. There in those schools we find the fire of evangelism touching the grass roots of our leadership for the future. The young people will come out of these schools with an understanding of the Program of Evangelism, and with all their youthful enthusiasm, dedication, and vigor, will help to promote it.

8. Nationally

It is from this program that other Baptist groups in America are joining with Southern Baptists in simultaneous crusades, covering the North American continent in a great year of evangelism in 1959.

9. Internationally

The influence of our Southern Baptist Program of Evangelism has gone far beyond our beloved nation. It has been appropriated by the National Baptist Convention, Incorporated, in the United States and also in Mexico, the countries of Latin America, and South America, with phenomenal and glorious results.

"What God Hath Wrought" is the subject of this book. The subject is not mis-stated nor are the claims in the contents of this book overestimated. For it is beyond the comprehension of finite man to evaluate such phenomena as have been discussed on the pages of this book. While God wrought all that has been done in his name, he used mortal man in doing it. Chief of these were the staff members of the Home Mission Board Department of Evangelism: Charley Matthews, secretary; C. Y. Dossey, assistant secretary; and associates E. Powell Lee, C. E. Autrey (now professor of Missions SWBTS), C. E. Wilbanks, and Eual Lawson. These men have been reinforced in their labors by the state secretaries of evangelism. The secretaries of evangelism have had the co-operation and help of every agency in the Southern Baptist Convention, the army of beloved pastors, and 30,000 churches in our Convention.

Programs do not save souls, but God-given programs are his means for bringing in his kingdom. God came to Southern Baptists in giving them the man about whom this book has been written, C. E. Matthews, and a program of evangelism for the Southern Baptist Convention.

This program of evangelism goes further than revivals. For 40 years the Home Board emphasis in evangelism has been upon revivals. Many marvelous Home Mission Board evangelists and singers had gone over the Convention territory conducting revivals. This program goes much further.

1. It is shot through and through with the teaching element:

in statewide conferences, associational clinics, fellowship clinics, soul-winning study courses and the new members class. This means permanency and continuity.

2. It promotes weekly visitation to the lost and unaffiliated professed Christians.

3. It promotes evangelistic music.

4. It builds an evangelistic church through the Church Council of Evangelism, using the church organizations and giving them the know-how. Thus it helps and uses the whole church membership. There is no way to evaluate the worth of this program as related to the movement to enroll "a million more in '54."

5. It is unique and different from any other program of evangelism known today. It fits as a perfect pattern into the mid-century life of Southern Baptist churches. It aids better revivals. It results in people joining the churches Sunday by Sunday, the year around. It strengthens every phase of church life. It keeps the pastor in his God-given place of spiritual leadership. It calls for no new organization in any church. It promotes and uses all of our Baptist literature and publicity. It is absolutely church centered. It magnifies the autonomy of the church, the autonomy of the pastor, and the autonomy of the program.

The soul of Charley Matthews in evangelism is crystallized, so far as could be done through his pen, in five books:

1. *Life's Supreme Decision*, 1941.

2. *The Department of Evangelism and the Simultaneous Revival Program*, 1946.

3. *The Southern Baptist Program of Evangelism*, 1949; revised 1952 and 1956.

4. *Every Christian's Job*, 1951.

5. *A Church Revival*, 1955.

Countless articles have gone from his pen for current publication in papers and periodicals.

With "Hats off to the past, coats off to the future," we joyfully exclaim, "WHAT GOD HATH WROUGHT THROUGH C. E. MATTHEWS!"

XIII

Family Sacrifice

From the day of the miraculous sale of their home, Charley and Nan were a unit in the Lord's will and work. Love and full accord filled the void left in his heart by his being orphaned.

Nan was queen of the home: mother, hostess to all church organizations, confidante of multitudes in sorrow and perplexity, and Charley's unfailing inspiration. She was a consistent soul-winner. Byron, Kathryn Louise, and Mary Elizabeth completed the circle of love.

Byron, law graduate from Baylor, is active in Travis Avenue Church. Mary Elizabeth, whose brilliance brought university scholarships and degrees, is now Mrs. L. A. Lomax and resides in Marshall, Texas. Byron, Jr. is a law student in Baylor. Little Kathryn Lomax is in grade school.

Kathryn Louise, deceased at age 11, remained an inspiration to all the family. Her Sunday school classroom, the Kathryn room, was a prayer room for the church. It was Charley's listening post where God met him and spoke. What God said there to Charley was followed and obeyed unswervingly.

A first cousin, Bernice Lacy Basham, twice hospitalized for tuberculosis, and supported by Charley and Nan, remained in closest affection, pride, and joy always.

The sacrifices paid as God wrought left Charley jobless when he resigned from Swift and Company and, again, from First Church, Fort Worth, to enter the seminary. Their hardships there have been recounted. While serving Travis Avenue Church, buildings, depression, and giving out always, brought him to his resignation $900.00 in debt, though his total income was about $10,000.00 per year in 1945-46.

He became secretary of evangelism in Texas at an estimated loss

128

of $3,000.00 per year, and further loss of $1,000.00 to go with the Home Mission Board to direct the Southern Baptist Program of Evangelism. In the face of this he left Travis Avenue treasury with $150,000.00 in cash and bonds for new buildings.

However, God recompensed. When Charley became secretary of evangelism for Texas Baptists, friends in Travis Avenue gave him a two-story, white, wooden residence, with four bedrooms and two baths, on three and a half rolling acres in Arlington. When it needed a roof one was put on as a gift. A Fort Worth layman gave him an air-conditioned Plymouth in 1955. In the spring of 1956, Bernice Basham, the cousin who would have died of tuberculosis but for Charley's help, now earning a handsome salary, redecorated the interior of the house. Here in this valuable home he recuperated from two heart attacks. He and Nan enjoyed their shade trees, shrubs, garden spots, and fruit trees. He summed it up to the writer: "God wrought it. In my total ministry I could not have saved enough money to buy this."

There was something else about the price which he paid, that he did not want people to know. First, he did not want people to know that from 1947 he had a heart condition known to medical science as angina. The cost of the sermons he preached was pain in his heart, physical pain which he often eased by taking a small tablet which he called nitroglycerin. He always slipped a tablet on the sly so that no one would know. The second great price, which finally cut him down, was another secret which he kept. The heart specialist told him after a thorough examination, "You have preached your heart out."

He had finished a revival crusade in Houston, Texas. However, Charley did not want his beloved wife, Nan, to know that he suffered an acute heart attack in the railroad station in Houston, November 25, 1954. He was putting her on a train to visit their daughter in Marshall, Texas. As he walked through the railroad station with her luggage, a pain almost dropped him to the floor. He slowed down and stopped at the gate to the passenger platform, and suggested that the trainmen would put her luggage on the train, and he would not go farther. She got on the train and left, not knowing that he had suffered a heart attack. It took him 20 minutes, moving slowly, stopping and sitting down, to get to his parked car across the street. Several times in the next few hours he thought he would die in his car en route home.

A few days following this date, he was to meet the heads of all the agencies of the Southern Baptist Convention, the Executive Committee and members of every board, in Nashville, Tennessee, to enlist their prayers, understanding, and full co-operation in the greatest evangelistic endeavor ever undertaken in Christian history. That December meeting was looking toward the simultaneous revival crusade which was to extend from the Atlantic to the Pacific and from Panama and Cuba to Alaska in 1955.

Against his doctor's counsel, he arose and appeared before scores of workers in Nashville at the appointed time. There were preliminary committee meetings. There was much discussion, and misunderstanding to be dealt with. There was great emotional expenditure on some whose hearts must be enlightened and warmed by the evangelistic fires in the heart of Charley Matthews. By the time he appeared at noon before a luncheon meeting of the entire number of men assembled in Nashville from over the Southern Baptist Convention territory, Charley was almost beyond standing. Yet no one knew, except a few associates who saw that his face was abnormally red with white splotches on his cheeks. He managed to address that group concerning the 1955 simultaneous revival crusade without one word about how he felt.

That afternoon he met his own staff and all the state secretaries of evangelism in their annual planning meeting. That meeting was more important than any other they had ever held, because the entire responsibility of the 1955 simultaneous crusades throughout the Southern Baptist Convention home mission territory must be considered and final plans perfected. Therefore, Charley managed to stay through that afternoon session, but said at the conclusion, "I will not be with you tomorrow."

He was a very sick man that night, and one of his associates, E. Powell Lee, ministered to him and got him on a plane to Fort Worth early the next morning. His constant appeal was, "Do not let anyone know about my heart condition. It might interfere with the progress of the 1955 Simultaneous Revival Crusade." That request was so honored and his illness kept so quiet that four months after the 1955 crusades the assistant executive secretary of the Home Mission Board said to the writer, "I did not know until now that Brother Matthews had suffered a heart attack. He must have kept it quiet lest it hurt the great simultaneous crusades."

He stayed at home, obeying his doctor's orders, trying to get his heart recuperated, for five long months. Then he came to the office once or twice weekly. His next public appearance was in the annual assembly at Glorieta in August, 1955. The price he had paid had kept him out of circulation from December to August. He was present in Glorieta to guide the work on the second revision of the book, *The Southern Baptist Program of Evangelism*, for the 1956 edition. He was encouraged to believe because of his activities, and not by the advice of his heart specialist, that he could conduct another revival meeting in September, following the Glorieta Assembly. Therefore, he and Mrs. Matthews drove to Linden, Texas, Saturday afternoon, September 25, for a single church revival.

The very next morning, the day he should have delivered his first sermon, as he and Mrs. Matthews were leaving the breakfast table, he exclaimed, "Oh, I have a severe pain," and sat down. By that time he was limp, and it was only the quick action of Mrs. Matthews in getting him into the town's hospital next door, and under an oxygen tent, that saved his life. He was there for days, and was returned to his home in Arlington in an ambulance. Thus he did "preach his heart out."

Ten months after his second heart attack he conducted an eight-day revival at Douglasville, Texas, in a little church of 40 members. So great was his desire to win people to Christ, that he gave evidence that he had rather die appealing to a lost person to come to his Saviour than to live a few months longer resting his heart and giving only counsel on evangelism. His great reward in this brief revival, was in witnessing the conversion of his little granddaughter, Kathryn.

Another great price which Brother Matthews paid, about which no one can intelligently speak, is the price of relinquishing his place as secretary of evangelism, promoting the Southern Baptist Program of Evangelism. Immediately following his second heart attack, the

Home Mission Board realized that almost a year of rest had not healed him. Therefore, the Board began searching for his successor and the mantle fell upon Dr. Leonard Sanderson, the brilliant secretary of evangelism in the state of Tennessee.

Before Dr. Sanderson arrived, January 1, 1956, Dr. Matthews came to his office at 516 Burt Building, Dallas, and loaded out his personal belongings from his desk. There was no fanfare and no sayings of farewells. His staff stood in the central office of the suite talking casually about the work, and he started shaking hands around with a smile on his face which belied the pain in his heart. The writer of these lines could not watch him go through the door, but stepped into his own office and shut the door. As Charley walked down the hallway to the elevator, the writer was saying to himself, "That's the longest walk that Charley has ever taken."

But Charley Matthews considered no price too great to be paid if one precious soul could be brought unto his Saviour. He believed that if a man drives a bad bargain in gaining the whole world and losing his own soul, then any Christian drives a worse bargain by saving his life and losing one soul which he might have brought to his Saviour.

Thus God has wrought in a man who has set a pattern in paying the price in soul-winning.

XIV

Charley's Gone Home

"Oh God, take me," was Charley's last prayer. These were also his last words. He spoke them after his beloved Nan had rushed him to the hospital from Mary Elizabeth's home in Marshall, Texas, on Friday afternoon, October 5, 1956, at 3:15, CST. All of us who lived and labored close to him tried to be in a state of preparation for his going, and at the same time hoped that it would be delayed.

On Sunday, September 23, Charley and Nan had the writer and his wife as dinner guests at Amon Carter Airport Restaurant to celebrate Mrs. Wilbanks' birthday. Charley looked well, visited all afternoon, and sought to dissuade us from leaving their residence when we did go home. He continued feeling well all week, and was anticipating with all eagerness a revival meeting in the Rose Hill Baptist Church in Texarkana, Arkansas.

His beloved Nan accompanied him to Texarkana where he met the official family of the church on Saturday night to perfect plans for the eight-day crusade. He returned to the room in a jubilant spirit, and Mrs. Matthews said she never saw him looking better.

Soon, however, severe pain hit him and it took three of his nitroglycerine tablets to bring any semblance of ease so he could last until they could get him to the hospital in Texarkana. He remained there until Tuesday afternoon, October 2, when he was permitted to lie down on an improvised bed on the back seat of his air-conditioned car and return to Mary Elizabeth's home in Marshall, Texas.

He seemed to continue improving, and was enthusiastic about the World Series baseball games. He watched that never-to-be-forgotten game Friday afternoon, as it came over television.

A few minutes after the game he became critically ill, and the right side of his face became red as blood. He did not speak, and

Mrs. Matthews said that she believed he had had a stroke. An oxygen-supplied ambulance got him to the hospital. Nothing could be done, for in a few minutes he said as best he could, "Oh God, take me," and was gone to be with his Lord. The body was in state in a funeral home in Fort Worth Sunday and Monday morning. Then it was viewed by his close friends and former church members in front of the pulpit in Travis Avenue Baptist Church between 1:00 and 2:00 o'clock.

At 2:30 o'clock Monday afternoon, October 8, Charley's pastor, Brother H. E. East, from First Baptist Church, Arlington; his successor in Travis Avenue Church, Pastor Robert (Bob) Naylor; and Dr. Robert G. Lee, pastor of Bellevue Baptist Church, Memphis, Tennessee, conducted the last rites. The great Travis auditorium was packed, and Charley's staff in the Department of Evangelism of the Home Mission Board were his pallbearers.

Pastor East paid brief tribute to Charley as a friend and church member. Pastor Naylor read the Scriptures, Romans 8:28-39, and led in prayer. A full choir of 40 voices, under the direction of Saxe Adams, sang two songs. All this was in literal keeping with Charley's written wishes. He had planned it all.

For the glory of his Redeemer and for the faith of all who were present, he had asked that the choir sing "My Saviour First of All." For the family's comfort the choir sang "Have Faith in God." Following the services the mile-long procession proceeded to the beautiful Mt. Olivet Cemetery between Fort Worth and Arlington, where Charley's body was laid to rest, awaiting the resurrection.

By previous and long-standing covenant between Dr. Matthews and Dr. Robert G. Lee, Dr. Lee brought the message. Had Dr. Lee gone home first, Dr. Matthews was to bring the message in his last rites.

It is most fitting that the man who wrote the introduction to this book should present to the readers a copy of the sermon as he reproduced it in writing following its delivery. Three weeks from the day the manuscript of this volume was finished and a copy placed in Charley's own hands, God wrought again in taking Charley home. Three days later God wrought a marvelous message through the lips of his distinguished servant, Dr. Robert G. Lee, as follows:

THE FUNERAL SERMON BY ROBERT GREENE LEE

One of the greatest honors of my life and one of the sweetest joys human heart could ever know was when by word of mouth and in words written with his pen, Dr. Matthews assured me, with comforting sweetness, of his love for me. Though we made no public declaration of it, my soul was knit with the soul of Charley Matthews —and I loved him as my own soul. And today I can say what David said of Jonathan: "Very pleasant hast thou been unto me; thy love to me was wonderful, passing the love of women" (2 Sam. 1:26).

I am here to speak these words today because of our agreement, our covenant, made a few years ago—the agreement that if I should die first he would speak at my funeral, and if he should die first, I would speak at his funeral.

With some affably serious levity, he asked me what I should say at his funeral. I told him I would not tell now what I would say then. Then I asked him what he would say at my funeral. He said: "Neither will I tell you what I shall say."

I remember when we made this agreement. We were flying over Los Angeles at night—descending for the landing. The myriads of lights beneath made a beautiful sight. I spoke of how little we knew of what went on beneath all the rooftops and on the boulevards and back alleys of that city. Then he spoke of what getting to heaven would be like—and we knew that more beautiful than any city of earth we could approach by plane or train or any other vehicle would heaven be—"the city which hath foundations whose maker and builder is God." As we were landing I quoted some verses from the 34th Psalm. And our promise as to death was made. It falls to me to do for him what he promised to do for me should I go first.

Once I was with him in this very house of God in a revival meeting—over 30 years ago. That was the first time I had the profit and pleasure of coming within the luminous shadow of this spiritual giant—fearless and faithful and zealous servant of God. He was a man who came as close as any man I have ever known to weighing 16 ounces to the pound on God's scales and measuring 36 inches to the yard by God's measuring rod. Day in and day out, at home and abroad, he struck 12 for God. And his greatness in the pulpit and out of the pulpit shows how God took a rill and made a strong-flowing and crystally-clear, deep river. His life shows how God took a candle and made a heaven-lit chandelier with a thousand glowing bulbs of splendor. His deeds testify as to how God took an acorn and grew a mighty oak. His earnest evangelistic fervor and success in revival meetings show how God took a whisper and brought it to a full voice for God. In evangelistic preaching and appeal his life was as an organ whose full voice was thunder—all keys beneath God's potent fingers pressed.

As proof of such a statement, I remind you that in Erick, Oklahoma, in 1927, there were 379 additions to the church, 251 for baptism upon confession of faith in the Son of God. In Electra, a little town in Texas, in 1928, there were 278 additions, 208 for baptism upon confession of faith in Christ. In Miami, Florida, at the Allapattah Baptist Church, in 1948, there were 356 additions to that church, 256 for baptism—and some baptized were Jews and some, Catholics. And in Red Bird, Missouri, he baptized 74 blood relatives—among whom were three brothers, one sister, and his grandmother.

I have wondered sometimes what, in years gone by, some would have said had they spoken at the funeral hour of some.

If Shem had spoken at the death of Noah who was a just and upright man in his generation and walked with God, he could have and would have spoken of him as a preacher of righteousness.

Had Lot spoken when Abraham's body was buried beside Sarah's, he could have spoken of Abram's wealth in character far beyond his wealth in cattle and sheep, in silver and gold.

Had Pharoah, who seemed to have been nursed on the tiger milk of cruelty, spoken when Joseph died at 110 years of age and his body put in a coffin in Egypt, the cruel king could have praised him as a godly statesman who blessed the whole land by taking famine fear from the heart of the nation.

Had Hur and Aaron spoken when Moses had angelic burial on lofty Nebo's brow, they could have given praise as high as the praise given by the writer of the book of Hebrews who spoke of him as one who chose "rather to suffer affliction with the people of God than to enjoy the pleasures of sin for a season—esteeming the reproaches of Christ greater riches than the treasures in Egypt, for he had respect unto the recompense of the reward."

Had some wise man spoken about Samuel when Samuel died, he could have spoken of how he washed the heart of Israel with the snow of high ideals.

Had all Israel spoken in eulogy when Joshua was buried in Mount Ephriam on the north side of the hill of Gaash, they would have said much about the valor and virtues of him who was a servant of the Lord.

Had Hilkiah, the priest, spoken at the funeral of Josiah, king of Judah, he would have told doubtless what is written in the Bible of him: "And like unto him was no king before him who turned to the Lord with all his might according to all the law of Moses."

Had Elisha spoken of Elijah after his departure—after there appeared a chariot of fire and parted them both asunder and Elijah went up by a whirlwind into heaven, he could have spoken of how this mighty man called an apostate nation back to God.

Had King Hezekiah spoken at the close of Isaiah's ministry, he could have told of how in his prophetic preaching there was the growl of the Assyrian wolf, God's instrument of judgment against his God-forsaking people, the thunders and lightnings of Sinai, and the crimson foregleams of Calvary.

Had someone spoken in eulogy over John the Baptist when his headless body was buried, he could have spoken of how he emptied the cities into the Jordan bottoms, as, in his preaching, he descended upon the iniquities of his day with a torch in one hand and a sword in the other—and how to him was given the very delicate task of interpreting the voice of betrothal as the friend of the bridegroom.

But they could have said nothing more in praise of these worthies of the olden days than we can say without exaggeration today of this mighty man by whom God wrought so marvelously in our Southern Baptist Convention and among other denominations who needed the warmth of evangelistic fires.

Truly we can say of him what was said of Caleb—that he followed the Lord fully. We say of him what was said of Barnabas: "He was a good man full of the Holy Ghost and of faith, and many people were added unto the Lord." Not only so. We can say of Dr.

Matthews what Paul said of himself: "For me to live is Christ." He, too, could say: "I am crucified with Christ: nevertheless I live; yet not I, but Christ liveth in me: and the life which I now live in the flesh by the faith of the Son of God, who loved me, and gave himself for me" (Gal. 2:20).

Had Titus, who accompanied Paul and Barnabas to the great council in Jerusalem, who was Paul's associate in evangelizing the isle of Crete—had he spoken of Paul, he could have spoken of how God revealed Jesus in Paul (Gal. 1:16). But write a chapter of Christian heroes as you will—and this great man's name will shine as brightly as many others—and his stature appears as tall as a symmetrical cedar of Lebanon. And his going from our Southern Baptist Convention is as when "a tall cedar falls and leaves a lonesome place against the sky."

I have been with Dr. Matthews on many occasions. I have been in long flights with him when planes were sometimes assaulted by storms. I traveled with him on trains when the whole land was encased in ice and snow was heavy upon the earth, and we were delayed by snow blockades. We have spoken from the same platforms. We have eaten at the same table. We have taken counsel together about our denominational affairs. We have agonized together, prayed together, laughed together, and, sometimes, we cried together. And thinking upon him and our togetherness in so many places, and on our evangelistic aims and hopes, I recall these words from the New Testament:

We are troubled on every side, yet not distressed; we are perplexed, but not in despair; persecuted, but not forsaken; cast down, but not destroyed; Always bearing about in the body of the dying of the Lord Jesus, that the life also of Jesus might be made manifest in our body. For we which live are alway delivered unto death for Jesus' sake, that the life also of Jesus might be made manifest in our mortal flesh (2 Cor. 4:8-11).

Dr. Matthews was a twice-born man. Born first, he was of clean-blooded parents. Born again, he was—"not of corruptible seed but of incorruptible by the Word of God." He knew what Jesus meant when he said "Ye must be born again" and "that which is born of the Spirit is spirit." Being born of the Spirit, he had in

138

his life the fruit of the Spirit "which is love, joy, peace, longsuffering, gentleness, goodness, meekness, faith, self-control."

He was twice a learner. Humble of spirit, never once in his life walking with the presumptuous step of a know-it-all, never having that superficial mental illumination that lacks the urge of sacrificial passion, he learned many things in school and many things in books he read. But he did what Jesus taught, who said: "Learn of me."

If he studied astronomy, he learned of Jesus, the Bright and Morning Star, the Sun of Righteousness, with healing in his wings. If he studied botany, he learned of him whose influence perfumed the stifling atmosphere of many areas as the Rose of Sharon. If he studied history, he learned of Jesus who is the supreme fact of all history. If he studied theology, he learned of Jesus who is the fundamental doctrine of theology. If he studied world conditions, he learned of him who is the only hope of a world that "looses wild tongues that hold not God in awe."

He was a possessor of two wisdoms—the wisdom of what true Baptists believe and the wisdom which is from above. Nothing could dilute his belief or lessen the strength of his declarations of all that true Baptists believe and of why they believe the things they do— and of why Baptists wrote history in blood before they wrote it in ink. But—praise God!—he did "shew out of a good conversation his works with meekness of wisdom" (James 3:13), and never had the wisdom which is "earthly, sensual, devilish" (James 3:15), but he had "the wisdom which is from above which is first pure, then peaceable, gentle, easy to be entreated, full of mercy, and good fruits, without partiality and without hypocrisy" (James 3:17).

Dr. Matthews had spiritual eyes for the two ways—"the wide gate and the broad way that leadeth to destruction," into which many enter, and "the straight gate and narrow way which leadeth unto life," the way which few find (Mat. 7:13-14). And he chose the right road, walking with God in that way in glad and grateful companionship —as did Enoch of old, having, as did Enoch, "this testimony that he pleased God" (Heb. 11:5).

There was in this great man's life the acknowledgment of two debts—his sin debt which Christ paid and the debt which he owed Christ. He believed and preached that Jesus paid all our sin debt—

not *some* of it nor *most* of it but *all* of it. He believed that if we had to pay even the least part of our sin debt that would make man a co-redeemer with Jesus which would be an absurdity. And he lived and loved and worked as though he owed all to Jesus. Sweet to him was the portion of that old hymn which says:

> Jesus paid it all, All to him I owe;
> Sin had left a crimson stain; He washed it white as snow.

In his life was the enriching illumination of two lights—the lights of the material universe and Jesus the Light of the world. He rejoiced in the light from the sun in his tabernacle in the heavens. He found delight in a night made glorious by the splendor of a full moon. He gazed in gratitude on occasions at the stars "the forget-me-nots of God blossoming in the infinite meadows of heaven." He knew that "there is one glory of the sun, and another glory of the moon and another glory of the stars"—and that "one star differeth from another star in glory" (1 Cor. 15:41). But better than this, he knew from experience what Jesus meant who said: "I am the light of the world; he that followeth me shall not walk in darkness, but shall have the light of life" (John 8:12).

He was the beneficiary of two blessednesses—the blessedness of sins forgiven and the blessedness of a Christian's triumphant death. Of one of these blessed realities the Psalmist spoke:

> Blessed is he whose transgression is forgiven, whose sin is covered. Blessed is the man unto whom the Lord imputeth not iniquity, and in whose spirit there is no guile (Ps. 32:1-2).

Of the other the great apostle John spoke when he wrote by the Holy Spirit these words:

> And I heard a voice from heaven saying unto me, Write, Blessed are the dead which die in the Lord from henceforth: Yea, saith the Spirit, that they may rest from their labors; and their works do follow them (Rev. 14:13).

In his Christian experience, in his Christian life and Christian death, Dr. Matthews had to do with two books—the Bible and the Book of Life.

The Bible he loved and believed. He never placed any question marks after any chapter or verse or word of it. He believed it to be the inspired, infallible, inerrant Word of God—universal in interest, immeasurable in influence, infallible in authority, regenerative in power, inspired in totality—the miracle book of diversity in unity, of harmony in infinite complexity. Would that all men today, that all young preachers who come after us and who will occupy our pulpits and have part in the matters of our Southern Baptist Convention life, would be always and everywhere as true to God's Word as was he.

But the other book I mention is spoken of by John in the Revelation—the book in which the names of the redeemed are written, the Book of Life:

And whosoever was not found written in the book of life was cast into the lake of fire (Rev. 20:15).

On the pages of that book "so bright and fair" his name was written—never to be erased.

But I would have you think of the two main friendships of his life—his friendship to God which he manifested, without variance or shadow or turning, and the friendship God manifested toward him. This was said of Abraham—in whom the glories of the Hebrew race were summarized: "Abraham believed God, and it was counted to him for righteousness; and he was called the Friend of God" (James 2:23). Such a statement could truthfully be made as to my gracious friend, the friend of so many, Dr. Matthews.

But he knew what a precious and enriching matter it was to have manifestations of friendship from God who could speak of him as he spoke of Abraham, noted for his close relations with God truly:

What a friend I've had in Jesus,
All my sins and griefs to bear.

But again, his Christian experience had to do with two homes— his earthly home and his heavenly home. In his earthly home he had the love of the precious wife of his bosom and of his children— and many times they took sweet counsel together—and knew how to lighten all loads and brighten all roads of home life. But, with a woeful sense of inadequacy oppressing me as I speak, I would have you think a moment of his heavenly home—the Father's house of many mansions in which Jesus had prepared for him a place. Beautiful home it is without griefs or graves, without disappointments or death, without sobs and tears, without sin and separations. "Eye hath not seen nor ear heard the things" God has prepared for him in that land where no shadow falls, where no slime is seen, where no funeral processions move, where no disease robs of health—and where praise of Jesus is the theme.

Now, I speak of the two monuments that can be built to his memory. We could build a monument of white marble which would speak of his clean life and of his "righteousness of God in Christ Jesus." We could build a monument of bronze and brass and stone. But the best monument we Southern Baptists, who will forever be indebted to him for his marvelous leadership in evangelistic endeavors, is the monument which moves in feet of flesh, works in hands of flesh, speaks in tongues of flesh, and beats in hearts of flesh carrying out his plans for evangelism through our churches—going forth to win men and women, boys and girls, to faith in Jesus Christ.

Southern Baptists should forever be grateful and prove their gratitude by lives utterly at the disposal of God—because of his life and preaching and leadership which touched every corner of our Convention territory—and many other areas of our land where functions our Southern Baptist Convention, the greatest evangelical body on the face of God's earth.

Dr. Matthews has written himself imperishably into the pages of our Southern Baptist Convention history—and indelibly into the hearts of multitudes who love the Christ he loved. His name is mentioned in little Baptist churches "up the creek," and out in remote corners and in village churches and in great city churches—and all over our nation.

Fruitfully he planted himself in the gardens of human hearts the land over. His daily life was a sermon. His conversations never left bitterness. He was free from the slavery of man's passions.

How every church in our Southern Baptist Convention should thank God that such a man was one of us—a man who, like Jesus, was so finely strung, so keyed to truth and justice and mercy and love, and so quickly felt the sorrow, the sympathy, and the indignation which wrong and injustice invariably elicit from all high souls. He was an author in life—writing the literature of godliness upon the fleshly tablets of human hearts. He loved God and people with his pocketbook as well as with his heart. And because he lived so well and loved so greatly and sacrificed so freely "many people were added unto the Lord"—and, being added, enlisted in the service of Jesus Christ through our churches.

And so, viewed from all angles, this hour is not defeat, but victory —not the end of life—because he that doeth the will of God abideth forever. I think of the poem Life and Death:

> From morn to eve they struggled
> Life and Death.
> At first it seemed to me as tho in mirth
> They contended—as foes of equal worth,
> But when the sharp red sun
> Cut through its sheath of Western clouds—
> I saw Death's grip tighten
> And bear the radiant form of life to earth.
> And suddenly both antagonists downward fell—
> And then—O, wonder of wonders,
> Marvel of marvels,
> When I went to the spot
> Where both antagonists had fallen,
> I could not find the body that I sought
> But one form was there—
> The dark, lone form of death!
> And it was dead!

So, today, I say:

> Adieu, sweet friend, you waited long
> For the voice that would call you home.
> And then it came like a low sweet note of joy
> Over the river's foam.
> And your heart shall ache,
> And your feet shall roam
> No more, no more. You have gone home.

Date Due

JAN 3 '66			
	PRINTED	IN U. S. A.	